THE
Hamburger
COMPANION

THE Hamburger COMPANION

A Connoisseur's Guide
to the Food We Love

DAVID GRAULICH

LEBHAR-FRIEDMAN BOOKS
NEW YORK

© 1999 David Graulich

Lebhar-Friedman Books
A company of Lebhar-Friedman Inc.
425 Park Avenue
New York, New York 10022

Library of Congress Cataloging-in-Publication data
Graulich, David J.
The hamburger companion : a connoisseur's guide to the food we love / David Graulich.
p.   cm.
ISBN 0-86730-762-5 (cloth : hc.)
1. Cookery (Beef). 2. Hamburgers—Anecdotes.
3. Cookery, American. I. Title.
TX749.5.B43G73 1999
641.6'62—dc21   98-55741
CIP

BOOK DESIGN AND COMPOSITION BY KEVIN HANEK
SET IN ADOBE MINION

Manufactured in the United States of America on acid-free paper
99 00 01 02 10   9 8 7 6 5 4 3 2 1

To my dad, Herbert Graulich,

who continues to lead by example

CONTENTS

CHAPTER 1 • The Hamburger Mystique   1

CHAPTER 2 • Hamburger Hyperbole   11

CHAPTER 3 • Hamburger History   19

CHAPTER 4 • They Also Serve   39

CHAPTER 5 • Local Legends   51

CHAPTER 6 • Secrets of the Burger-Meisters   65

CHAPTER 7 • Burgers and Billionaires   75

CHAPTER 8 • Pop Goes the Burger   81

CHAPTER 9 • The Raw and the Cooked   99

ACKNOWLEDGMENTS   111

PHOTO CREDITS   113

INDEX   115

THE
Hamburger
C O M P A N I O N

✳ *Chapter One* ✳

THE HAMBURGER MYSTIQUE

*I*F HAMBURGERS WERE only a food, I wouldn't be writing this book. Hamburgers are far more than something to eat. Hamburgers transcend the boundaries of the grill, the microwave, the luncheon plate, or the dinner table. Hamburgers are the anchor of a culinary trinity that is the All-American meal: burger, french fries, and a milk shake. To food writer Sharon Tyler Herbst, hamburgers are "edible institutions."

Celebrated in art and literature, a fabled icon of popular culture, an eagerly sought roadside attraction, a source of comfort whether we're home or in strange surroundings, the hamburger is a classic American hero—modest, steady, and reliable. If a movie biography of the hamburger had been made in the 1940s, the starring role would have gone to Henry Fonda, Jimmy Stewart, or Gary Cooper. Like those actors, hamburgers are plain-spoken, unpretentious, and good to have with you if caught in a tough spot.

When people talk about favorite hamburgers, they express themselves with fervor, enthusiasm, and passion. Their eyes sparkle, and

Hamburgers transcend the boundaries of the grill,
the microwave, the luncheon plate, or the dinner table

they wave their hands and arms to simulate the burger's preparation, arrival, and consumption. Their words convey an exquisite sense of the hamburger's taste and heft, the crunch and texture of the bun, the visceral experience of holding the burger in both hands and getting the mouth wide open. Clearly, this is not a food to be delicately pecked at by a nonpartisan nibbler. Here's how Bob Irving of Pacifica, California, describes his favorite hamburger at Tommy's, located in the old Gold Rush town of McCloud, California, at the foot of Mount Shasta:

"the Golden Arches of McDonald's... like beacons in the night."

The first time I went in and ordered a Tommy-burger, I didn't know what it was. I saw a three-quarter-pound hamburger, a gigantic hamburger with a special bun made for it. The burger is on one plate, and a huge pile of fries is on another plate; it was like having a little Mount Shasta of fries. I'm drooling because I didn't have breakfast that morning. I start eating the hamburger, and the juice is running down both arms; I'm holding it in both hands. It is a very, very good hamburger, it knocks you out, it's the kind where you should leave enough time to take a nap afterwards.

Other writers strive to capture the hamburger mystique. John Mariani, in his book *America Eats Out,* refers to "the Golden Arches of McDonald's, as familiar and beckoning as the Statue of Liberty, like beacons in the night." Providing a British perspective, *The Economist* declares that "the rise of the hamburger is a metaphor for the rise of America. Like the immigrants

themselves, the hamburger evolved in the New World.... the hamburger is triumphant." "A hamburger," says novelist Tom Robbins, "is warm and fragrant and juicy... soft and non-threatening.... A hamburger is companionable and faintly erotic."

In his book *Made in the U.S.A: The Secret Histories of the Things that Made America*, Phil Patton muses on the convergence of forces behind the all-conquering hamburger:

> The hamburger aspired to be the universal American food. It was beef, the most favored of American foods. It was portable and required no utensils. It could be customized with the addition of various toppings and garnishes. It was easy to cook, even by the unskilled.
>
> The hamburger was fun—it was sports food, just as there are sports clothes and sports cars. Covered with ketchup and onions, it played out the same cheap melodramatics of salt and sugar, bitter and sweet, that appeal to the American palate.... The burger itself, garnished with tomato, onion, and lettuce, and sandwiched between bun halves, replicates the whole meat/starch/vegetable division in a neat assembly.

We'll view the hamburger with the discriminating eye of the connoisseur...

Yet for all the familiarity and down-home earthiness of the hamburger, the simple actions of ordering and eating it remain a special sort of treat. Adrian Bonnar is owner and operator of Bistro Burger, a restaurant in San Francisco's Financial District. He sees his lunchtime customers order green salads and grilled chicken early in the week. As Thursday and Friday roll around, says Bonnar, his hamburgers sales increase by

30 percent or more: "By Friday office workers feel they deserve a reward. They've worked hard all week, and they're in a good mood and looking ahead to the weekend. That's when they order a hamburger."

Burger devotion extends beyond the masses; it thrives among cooking's elite. Marcel Desaulniers is owner and executive chef of the Trellis Restaurant in Williamsburg, Virginia, and author of *The Burger Meisters,* a dazzling compendium of recipes from 47 master chefs. "I am amazed at how often food conversations with my colleagues invariably turn from what is 'in' to what is personally preferred," Desaulniers writes in *The Burger Meisters.* "The food most widely proclaimed as the choice away from work is a burger."

...evaluating its culinary aspects as well as its cultural and industrial achievements.

This book is an appreciation of the hamburger—a consideration of its merits and history, a celebration of its virtues and contributions. We'll view the hamburger with the discriminating eye of the connoisseur, evaluating its culinary aspects as well as its cultural and industrial achievements.

To be sure, the hamburger has its share of critics. Some nutritionists see it as an abomination. Others attack it as a flagship of American imperialism, corporate arrogance, and overseas exploitation. When manifested as the mainstay of fast-food restaurants, neighborhood activists often protest the hamburger's proposed entry into a community. For all of the devotion, affection, and love that it inspires among its admirers, the basic burger is, at times, an embattled burger.

There are even those whose antagonism is inflamed because of semantic allegations. Food historians Waverley Root and Richard de Rochemont fumed in 1976: "The fact that 'hamburger' has given rise to

writer, M.F.K. Fisher, related a nostalgic anecdote in *The Art of Eating* (1954):

When I was much younger and proportionately hungrier and less fin-

senseless words like 'cheeseburger' is one of the many signs which betray the increasing degeneration of the American language."

Admittedly, some of us go through a love-hate thing with the hamburger. America's most celebrated food

icky, a minor form of bliss was going to a drive-in near school and eating two or three weird, adulterated combinations of fried beef, mayonnaise, tomato catsup, shredded lettuce, melted cheese, unidentifiable relish, and sliced onion. These concoctions were called "Rite-Spot Specials," in dubious honor of the place that served them. They seemed wonderful then. Now I gag.

It is beyond the modest scope of this work to respond to those who are philosophically, aesthetically, nutritionally, or politically opposed to the hamburger. Similarly, we will make no attempt to consider the nonbeef variations of the hamburger that are now in the market—veggie burgers, grain burgers, soy burgers, turkey burgers, and the like. These semi-hemi-demi-burgers reside in an elevated province of their own, paragons of culinary rectitude and dietetic correctness.

This will be a sentimental journey through the halls of unabashed hamburger devotion.

Instead, this will be a sentimental journey through the halls of unabashed hamburger devotion. I remember eating a hamburger for lunch in Cleveland, Ohio, along the frozen shores of Lake Erie during the bleak winter of 1976. I was in my first job after college, far from home and thoroughly miserable. Hamburger was the house special of the restaurant near the office, and it was about the only item I recognized on the menu (remember, I was just out of college). The hamburger was a comrade in an otherwise unhappy landscape.

On a happier note, I recall a hamburger in Knoxville, Tennessee, when I was visiting that college town with my wife, Rebecca, in 1992. The restaurant was a cheerful pub filled with University of Tennessee students. Enjoying a hearty, stacked-to-the-sky burger with fries, washed down with a cold beer, and followed by apple pie and coffee, we were transported back to college times, except that we didn't have to write any term papers. I also recall three hamburgers eagerly eaten at an American fast-food restaurant in Hong Kong, when we were at the end of a three-week Asian vacation, and I desperately craved a familiar taste after too many chicken-rice-and-noodle repasts.

One pleasant surprise of my research was that I discovered how much good writing exists about hamburgers—writing that is colorful and evocative. I will quote at length from some of these accounts. Furthermore, a considerable amount of American history is woven through the hamburger chronicles: the immigrant experience, the emergence of the suburbs and the interstate highways, the development of a service-sector economy that surpassed the manufacturing sector, the response of the food industry to the popularity of the hamburger, and the explosion of franchising as a form of wealth creation and entrepreneurship.

That's a lot to ask from a seasoned ground-beef patty on a bun—but that is the story that awaits us.

Chapter Two

HAMBURGER HYPERBOLE

*T*HE IMMENSITY OF THE hamburger's popularity has inspired its own form of statistical expression. Huge numbers and mind-boggling metaphors convey the enormity of the burger phenomenon.

Fred Turner, the former chief executive of McDonald's, used to refer to this as "burgers-to-the-moon publicity." As journalist John F. Love explains in his book *McDonald's: Behind the Golden Arches,* McDonald's is a masterful and creative hypeologist, from its original "Millions Sold" signage to its proclamations

announcing that total ketchup sold in a given year could fill Lake Michigan, or that its burgers could stretch to the moon (or Saturn or Mars) and back many times.

Hamburgers lend themselves to fanciful statistics. *Time* magazine got into the fun-with-numbers game in its 1973 cover story on McDonald's, when it gushed that the 12 billion hamburgers McDonald's had sold could "form a pyramid 783 times the size of the one erected by Snefu."

I don't know who Snefu was or whether he or she ate hamburgers, but that really doesn't matter. Ham-

Huge numbers and mind-boggling metaphors convey the enormity of the burger phenomenon

Burger Facts at a Glance...

- 38 percent include ketchup
- 30 percent include mustard
- 28 percent include cheese
- 21 percent include onion
- 20 percent include mayonnaise/salad dressing
- 20 percent include tomatoes
- 19 percent include lettuce
- 17 percent include pickles
- 4 percent include relish
- 2 percent include BBQ sauce

burgers and numbers go well together. Hamburger numerology manages to be impressive, fabulous, and utterly meaningless, all at the same time.

Being a true hamburger companion requires a journey along the hallways of burger numerology. Think of it as the equivalent of the weekend box-office figures released by Hollywood or the ceaseless stream of statistics (number of fumbles by left-handed quarterbacks on third down) during *Monday Night Football.*

The Economist reported in 1997 that the number of hamburgers and cheeseburgers consumed in U.S. restaurants "jumped by nearly a fifth since 1990." The magazine continues its analysis: "The average American eats three hamburgers a week, a collective effort that puts paid to 40 billion burgers annually." Getting warmed up and more into the true hyperbolic spirit, *The Economist* explains that "McDonald's has served 70 billion hamburgers, enough to reach to the moon and back 17 times."

A splendid source of burger-based statistics is the National Cattlemen's Beef Association. For example, the chart on the previous page shows the hierarchy of toppings Americans choose to have with their burger.

The Cattlemen's Association also has studied burger preferences, resulting in the rather inappropriately named pie chart (below) that shows

"Regular hamburger" slightly in the lead, ahead of "Large Cheeseburger."

Here are more statistical tidbits and ground-beef factoids that have been gathered from the collective wisdom of pollsters, industry surveys, and however else unusual statistics are generated:

- Large cheeseburgers are a fast-growing choice, with orders increasing 7 percent in 1997 over 1996.

- One-third of all Americans have eaten a hamburger or some form of ground beef in the past 24 hours.

- Hamburgers appear on 73 percent of all foodservice menus.

Hardee's Monster Burger boasts five ounces of hamburger, three slices of cheese, eight strips of bacon, and plenty of mayonnaise. In 1997 the chain introduced the Grilled Sourdough Patty Melt, with an eight-ounce patty, cheese, and

HAMBURGER PREFERENCES

(Source: 1997 NPD/CREST, National Cattlemen's Beef Association)

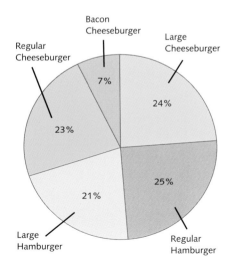

Above: With 5 ounces of hamburger, three slices of cheese, eight strips of bacon, and plenty of mayonnaise, Hardee's Monster Burger is aptly named

Right: 1997 advertisement announcing Hardee's Grilled Sourdough Patty Melt

grilled onions on sourdough bread, weighing in at 600 calories and 34 fat grams.

In 1970, in response to a meat shortage, General Mills introduced a pasta-and-seasoning boxed addi-

HAMBURGER CONSUMPTION BY REGION
(Source: 1997 NPD/CREST, National Cattlemen's Beef Association)

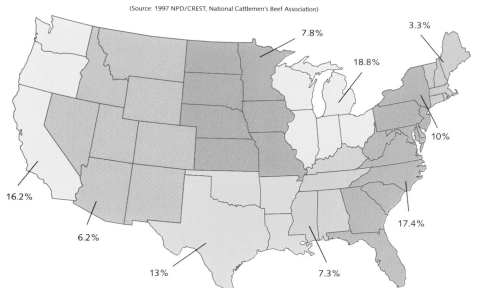

Hamburgers and cheeseburgers make up 76.5 percent of all beef consumed away from home. Prime rib weighs in at a measly 2.9 percent.

People in the North Central and South Atlantic regions consume the most burgers (see chart above).

tive called Hamburger Helper, so that a homemaker could stretch a single pound of hamburger into a meal for five. America's inflationary economy during the 1970s made the product a winner with budget-conscious cooks. Hamburger Helper spawned a brood of pasta-or-rice-based products for ground beef, including Hamburger Helper Creamy Mushroom with Noodles, Hamburger Helper Cheeseburger Macaroni, Hamburger Helper Rice Oriental Dinner, and Hamburger Helper Tacobake dinner.

Phil Patton, author of *Made in the U.S.A.,* filed this report from the epicenter of hamburger hyperbole:

Some years ago, I was invited to the ceremonial frying of the 50 billionth McDonald's hamburger. The event took place in the great ballroom of a New York hotel, all gilt and draperies. In the middle stood a single, simple grill, like an altar. Onto the grill was deposited the pale pink, round disc—exactly 1.6 ounces in weight, 3.875 inches in diameter—of the official burger. The company president, who began as a frycook, held up the patty for the television cameras in a way (insinuating delicacy and value) that reminded me of a round wafer of silicon onto which computers are printed and then, a moment later, of the priest's symbolic elevation of the Host. Or perhaps a disc of nuclear fuel.

The exact timing of the event partook of some license, since it could only be estimated, by time, from the production figures of McDonald's outlets around the world. At that minute, determined to be 12:05 EST, the patty was placed on the grill. With a flourish of drumbeats and marching-band music, the slightly reticulated patty was fried and deposited on a bun.

Chapter Three

HAMBURGER HISTORY

*L*IKE MANY AMERICAN classic products, the origins of the hamburger are shrouded in controversy. Just as the invention of the telephone and the integrated circuit are hotly contested, credit for the hamburger is debated by rival factions.

Where did the hamburger begin? Some authorities claim that Italian physicians as far back as 780 A.D. were prescribing chopped beef fried with onions to cure colds and coughs. According to a restaurateur and writer named Ronald L. McDonald—a name that commands respect in hamburger circles—the food began with nomadic warrior horsemen, racing out of Asia into Eastern Europe. Their leader was a culinary *bon vivant* named Temujin, also known as Genghis Khan. In an inspired and fanciful depiction of the hamburger's origins, McDonald writes:

Beginning in the 13th century, an army of fierce horsemen that conquered everyone and every nation in its path, rolled across the steppes of Asia. The Mongol riders needed food that could be carried on their mounts

What's in a name: In one of those frequent semantic oddities that shows up in the food business, the vague connection between the city of Hamburg and the burger has stuck

and eaten easily with one hand while they rode.... Ground meat was the perfect choice for the Mongols. They could use scrappings of lamb, which were formed into flat patties. They placed these uncooked patties in rolled skins and carried them under their saddle until it was time to eat. The constant pressure mashed the meat between the saddle and the horse, tenderizing it as they rode.

It remains unclear whether Genghis Khan was a cheeseburger type or preferred, say, a medium-rare, saddle-mashed lamb burger with yogurt.

The hamburger lineage resumes in the Baltic countries of Finland, Estonia, and Latvia, where ground beef was seasoned with salt, pepper, and onion juice. The delicacy spread to the German port city of Hamburg, where German chefs livened up the dish with pickles, eggs, and chopped sardines. "It was during the era of global expansion in the 1600s," declares Ronald L. McDonald, "that today's true hamburger was born."

Most historians agree that European immigrants brought the concept of the hamburger to America with them during the 19th century, enlarging what *The New York Times* referred to as "the great hamburger Diaspora." The vague connection with the city of Hamburg remained, in one of those frequent se-

It remains unclear whether Genghis Khan was a cheeseburger type or preferred, say, a medium-rare, saddle-mashed lamb burger with yogurt.

mantic oddities that shows up in the food business. In John F. Love's chronicle of McDonald's ascendancy, *Behind the Arches,* he records an existentialist moment in the 1960s when McDonald's arranged a publicity stunt with the mayor of Hamburg to celebrate the "return" of the hamburger to its native city. "What is *this* hamburger?" asked the mayor. "*I* am a Hamburger."

The next milestone is the year 1834, with the appearance of "hamburger steak" on the menu of Delmonico's Restaurant at 494 Pearl Street in lower Manhattan. Along with a hamburger steak for 10 cents, a Delmonico's patron could enjoy soup for two cents, a slice of pie for four cents and a cup of tea or coffee for one cent.

A 19th-century British physician named James Henry Salisbury recommended that everyone eat ground beef three times a day as a preventative against colitis, anemia, asthma, rheumatism, and tuberculosis. Dr. Salisbury wrote in 1888

that "man is about two-thirds carnivorous and one-third herbivorous. Our stomach is designed to digest lean meat." The good doctor's prescriptions have a legacy today on many menus—the chopped lean beef known as a Salisbury steak. During World Wars I and II, when German-sounding names fell into disfavor in the United States, many restaurants used Salisbury steak as a *nom de guerre.*

A considerable controversy rages regarding who invented the modern American hamburger. Jeffrey Tennyson, in his book *Hamburger Heaven,* relates the story of 15-year-old Charlie Nagreen of Seymour, Wisconsin, who in 1885 slipped butter-fried ground beef between slices of bread at the Outgamie County fair. Charlie's customers could stroll the fairgrounds as they ate. No flash-in-the-pan, Nagreen became known as "Hamburger Charlie" and served buttered burgers at the county fair for the next 65 years. In 1989 the town of Seymour

Seymour, Wisconsin
"The Home of the Hamburger"

Seymour, Wisconsin, resident Charles "Hamburger Charlie" Nagreen (left), who slipped butter-fried ground beef between slices of bread at the 1885 Outgamie County fair, so that customers could stroll the fairgrounds as they ate. Above, scenes from the town's 1989 hamburger extravaganza, including the ketchup slide (top left) and the world's largest hamburger (above right), weighing in at 5,520 pounds and measuring 21 feet in diameter.

commemorated its place in culinary history by cooking "The World's Largest Hamburger." It weighed 5,520 pounds and was 21 feet in diameter.

Credible competing claims to the title "Father of the Hamburger" are made by the descendants of Louis Lassen of New Haven, Connecticut; Frank Menches of Akron, Ohio; and Fletcher "Old Dave" Davis of Athens, Texas. Molly O'Neill, food writer for *The New York Times,* favors the Menches theory, which postulates that in 1892 a 27-year-old food vendor nearly ran out of sausages and began grinding them into patties to extend his supply. O'Neill admits a bias because she is from Ohio: "The Akron version allows me to feel that burgers and I are cut from the same cloth. This is not a pretty image, I grant you. But when you're dealing with icons, beauty, like facts, is beside the point."

The ferris wheel at the 1904 World's Fair in St. Louis, where the hamburger was established as an American classic

In the authoritative book *The Food Chronology,* James Trager cites the 1904 World's Fair in St. Louis as establishing the hamburger as a standard American classic. "[In 1904] the chopped beef specialty is fried and sold by German immigrants living in South St. Louis," Trager writes.

The hamburger was perfectly primed, so to speak, for the advent of the automobile. As Americans took to the road, the hamburger was the food of choice, whether for the hungry commuter or the Sunday afternoon recreational driver. Jeffrey Tennyson refers to restless, energetic Americans in search of "the hasty and the tasty," and the automobile and the hamburger began one of the most tightly woven, lucrative, and dynamic dual relationships in business history.

By the 1930s, hamburger stands were a fixture of roadside America. In John Steinbeck's *The Grapes of Wrath,* the Joad family leaves the Oklahoma Dust Bowl and drives along Route 66 to California, making stops at gasoline stations with adjoining eateries. Steinbeck's prose still stands as a practical guide to the exquisite art of preparing and cooking a hamburger:

Along 66 the hamburger stands—Al & Susy's Place—Carl's Lunch—Joe & Minnie—Will's Eats.... the cook is Joe or Carl or Al, hot in a white coat and apron.... Wiping the griddle, slapping down the hamburger.... He presses down a hissing hamburger with his spatula. He lays the split buns on the plate to toast and heat. He gathers up stray onions from the plate and heaps them on the meat and presses them in with the spatula. He puts half the bun on top of the meat, paints the other half with melted butter, with thin pickle relish. Holding the bun on the meat, he slips the spatula under the thin pad of meat, flips it over, lays the buttered half on top, and drops the hamburger on a small plate. Quarter of a dill pickle, two black olives beside the sandwich. Al skims the plate down the counter like quoit. And he scrapes the griddle with the spatula and looks moodily at the stew kettle.

THE CORPORATE ERA DAWNS

The industrial history of the hamburger starts with the White Castle chain. Indeed, a great deal of hamburger history is embedded within this company, which remains a prosperous firm and has gained cult status.

Two entrepreneurs in Wichita, Kansas, started White Castle in 1921. Edgar Waldo "Billy" Ingram was a local insurance and real-estate agent, and Walter Anderson was a professional cook. They met when Ingram sold Anderson a house. The two men developed a distinctive way of cooking a flattened hamburger, with shredded onions, and introduced a catchy slogan: "Buy 'em by the Sack."

White Castle made numerous contributions to the popularity of

John Steinbeck's description of roadside hamburger stands like the one at left, in his novel *The Grapes of Wrath*, remains the classic portrayal of this piece of culinary Americana. Below, a scene from the 1940 motion picture version of the Steinbeck story.

the hamburger. The company modeled its stores after Chicago's famous Water Tower, and the distinctive architecture would inspire many other hamburger design motifs. Ingram and Anderson insisted on cleanliness and hygiene and helped dispel public fears about the safety of the hamburger.

From its Midwestern base, White Castle's hamburgers built a huge following of fans, who dubbed its burgers with affectionate nicknames like "belly sliders." The chain had battalions of imitators, as recorded by hamburger historian Jeffrey Tennyson: White Tower, White Hut, White Manna, White Clock, White Dome, White Diamond, White Crests, White Cups, White Palaces, White Taverns,

White Midgets, White Spots, Royal Castles, Kings Castles, Blue Castles, Silver Castles.

An Internet site (www.shadow.net/~colbert/story/stories) collects testimonials from White Castle fans, such as this tribute from 57-year-old Len O., a resident of Washington, D.C., who grew up in Chicago:

While on a trip to Chicago recently, I stopped in a White Castle and ordered 200 White Castles to go (I planned this ahead of time and had several collapsible carry-on bags with me just for this purpose). A young high-school girl behind the counter did not believe me and thought I was pulling her leg. After several minutes of trying to convince her that I was serious, the manager came out to see what the discussion was about. It was then that I took out over $100 from my wallet, laid it on the counter, and told the manager that I wanted 200 hamburgers to go. The manager needed no further convincing nor encouragement. Suddenly two more people appeared from the kitchen, and a production line quickly was set up to cook, box, and package 200 hamburgers.

After leaving the White Castle restaurant, while in the parking lot for the rental-car return, I transferred the 200 hamburgers to four zippered carry-on bags for my flight back to Washington, D.C. Upon boarding the plane, I placed the carry-on bags in the overhead compartment. Shortly after takeoff, I began to smell the White Castle aroma emanating from the overhead compartment. I tried to ignore it but soon noticed other passengers were smelling my hamburgers, and I could overhear several conversations concerning the aroma. Most of the people thought that the aroma was our airline dinner being heated up.... Upon arrival in Washington, I opened the overhead compartment, and the aroma from the White Castles was suddenly overwhelming. Everyone around me started laughing and making wise comments—two were even applauding. A stewardess kidded me that my hamburgers smelled better than the airline dinner entrée. In the baggage claim area I was the butt of many good-natured comments. I could not get out of that airport fast enough!

The tiny hamburger with the giant legion of fans: "Buy 'em by the Sack"

Richard G. adds:

I live near Boston, and I replenish my freezer's Whitey-One-Bite supply every few months. I created an insulated box by lining a large computer monitor box with 1-inch rigid foam. I check it, mostly empty, as luggage on the plane when I'm flying to Chicago. On the day I depart, I stop by a White Castle, fill the box with frozen Sliders, and check it as luggage back to Boston. Works perfectly.

Finally, there's this romantic tale from George O.:

My wife and I met about five years ago at a Cornell reunion party. Our first conversation revolved around our fascination for those beautiful, five-holed, square, tasty, steamed burgers. I knew immediately she was the woman for me. Today, we walked from Manhattan to Queens over the Queensborough Bridge to the nearest White Castle. It's at least three miles, and the bridge was covered with snow. It was definitely worth the trip; we had a great time. Of course, the restaurant was full of the standard wackos that make it all the more interesting. I've got a million other White Castle stories. Great to see that others are as crazy about White Castle as I am.

The McDonald's story has entered the folklore of American business: A milk-shake machine salesman named Ray Kroc journeys from Chicago to see why a hamburger stand in San Bernadino, California, is using phenomenal numbers of milk-shake machines. He discovers that two brothers named Maurice McDonald and Richard McDonald, originally from New Hampshire, are running a gold mine, selling 15-cent hamburgers, 10-cent french fries, and many, many milk shakes. The first McDonald's mascot was a cartoon figure called Speedee, who was obliged to take early retirement when he was found to have an unfortunate resemblance to the mascot for Alka-Seltzer. These excerpts from a 1952 magazine advertisement demonstrated the McDonald brothers' minimalist philosophy as well as their feisty New England humor:

The Most Important 60 Seconds
in Your Entire Life!

Imagine—No Cars Hops—
No Waitresses—No Waiters—
No Dishwashers—No Bus Boys

The McDonald's System
is Self Service

No More Glassware—No More
Dishes—No More Silverware

The McDonald's System Eliminates All of This!

Complete Plans Are Now Available.

We Promised It Would Take 60 Seconds To Read This. The 60 Seconds Are Now Up.

It took a long time for McDonald's—and, by proxy, other fast food—to be taken seriously by their peers in the establishment business world. In 1983 Theodore Levitt of the Harvard Business School wrote one of the first appreciative evaluations, from a management perspective, of what the McDonald's system had achieved:

Like Henry Ford's Model T, McDonald's owes much of its success to the conscious design of an industrial system productive enough to offer abundance and quality at bargain-basement, customer-attracting prices.

McDonald's represents the industrialization of service...

That was its original goal, and that has been its spectacular achievement. It was no accident.

Raw hamburger patties are carefully premeasured and prepackaged in a capital-intensive central commissary, thus leaving neither the franchisee nor his employees any discretion as to size, quality, or consistency.... Each outlet's storage and preparation space and related facilities are expressly designed for, and limited to, a predetermined mix of products.

The tissue to wrap each hamburger is color-coded to denote the mix of condiments. Heated reservoirs hold prepared hamburgers for rush demand. Frying surfaces have spatter guards to prevent soiling of the cooks' uniforms. Nothing is left to chance or

Ray Kroc, whose vision turned the McDonald's franchise into one of the legendary success stories of American entrepreneurship

32

the employees' discretion. The entire system is engineered and executed according to a tight technological discipline that ensures fast, clean, reliable service in an atmosphere that gives the modestly paid employees a sense of pride and dignity.

McDonald's represents the industrialization of service, applying through management the same systematic modes of analysis, design, organization, and control that are commonplace in manufacturing.

The original McDonald's formula remains effective today. In California a chain called In-N-Out Burger has built a fanatical following by offering a limited menu, low prices, fast service, and fresh-cut fries and freshly ground burgers.

Another characteristic of the McDonald brothers that is striking, almost 50 years after the fact, is the reason that they sold out to Kroc. The two brothers didn't like to fly, they didn't enjoy being away from home, and they basically had as much money as they needed to live a pleasant Southern California life. That sounds unbelievable in the go-go 1990s, but it's true. Richard McDonald died in 1998 (Maurice died in 1971), and in his *New York Times* obituary he was quoted on why he didn't aspire to commanding a national franchise empire: "I would have wound up in some skyscraper somewhere with about four ulcers and eight tax attorneys trying to figure out how to pay all my income tax."

If McDonald's is the Coca-Cola of the hamburger industry—the dominant global brand—then Burger King is the Pepsi. Two graduates of Cornell's School of Hotel Administration, James McLamore and David Edgerton, were running a small Florida operation during the mid-1950s, then called Insta-Burger King. McLamore described in his autobi-

The Whopper became the single best-selling sandwich in the foodservice industry and transformed Burger King from a struggling Florida chain into an international powerhouse

ography how he and Edgerton visited one of their struggling outlets in Gainesville, Florida, near the University of Florida campus, in 1957. McLamore wandered down the street from his money-losing unit and discovered a fabulously successful local burger joint. The two men experienced an epiphany while they were driving home, marking yet another great moment in the symbiosis of automobiles and hamburgers:

The [nearby] restaurant was run down and dirty and the appearance of their service personnel left a lot to be desired. The place was a mess, but I kept looking at the long lines of customers waiting to buy their food. I had to know why these people were crowding the place when 100 yards down the street at the new Burger King, we had absolutely no business.

I ordered two hamburgers.... I unwrapped this big hamburger and saw that it consisted of a quarter-pound hamburger patty on a big 5-inch bun served with lettuce, tomatoes, mayonnaise, pickles, onions, and catsup. After a few bites, it wasn't hard to understand why these customers were carrying them out by the bag. The hamburger was big, and it tasted great.

On the drive back to Miami, the two partners talk about how an oversized hamburger could be the breakthrough product:

Dave always did the driving on our many trips around the state, and because it was late in the afternoon, I decided it was cocktail time. I had a small bottle of bourbon in the glove compartment, so I poured a little of it into a 7-Up I had just bought at the gas station. All I could think about was that big, good-tasting hamburger I had just eaten.... I suggested that we call our product a Whopper, knowing that this would convey imagery of something big. I also suggested that we put signs reading "Home of the Whopper" under our Burger King name to indicate that our new product was the specialty of the house.... The idea of introducing the Whopper was all we could talk about. We arrived in Miami long after midnight, tired but excited about our plans to add the Whopper to our menu.

The Whopper became the single best-selling sandwich in the foodservice industry and transformed Burger King from a struggling Florida chain into an international powerhouse. A helipad in London used to call itself the "Whopper Chopper" and served its namesake burgers to pilots; and until recently strollers in Paris could see signs that proudly proclaimed "Maison du Whopper" along the Champs-Élysées.

James W. McLamore (right), co-founder of the Burger King chain, pictured in front of an early Burger King unit in Florida, virtually unchanged from its original appearance (top)

Chapter Four

THEY ALSO SERVE

It was all for the customer, to let him know we cared.
— BOB WIAN, FOUNDER OF BOB'S BIG BOY

C DONALD'S AND Burger King are the Big Two, but they have plenty of competition from regional and national chains that are built around the burger. Here's a look at several of these burger barons:

Wendy's

He's fostered an image in television commercials as a bumbler who's a little slow on the take, but don't let that fool you. In real life R. David "Dave" Thomas is a driven, talented entrepreneur who rose from hum-ble beginnings to build a $2 billion international corporation traded on the New York Stock Exchange.

Thomas began working in food-service at a Knoxville, Tennessee, lunch counter at the age of 12. He dropped out of high school after his sophomore year although he earned his degree as an adult. Following an army stint, he took over a bankrupt Kentucky Fried Chicken franchise in Columbus, Ohio, and rapidly turned the business around. One of his tactics was trading radio commercial airtime in exchange for buckets of chicken.

R. David "Dave" Thomas, the founder of Wendy's, in one of the chain's television commercials, which have made him one of the most recognized faces in fast food

Thomas with the real-life inspiration for the name of his chain, daughter Wendy

Thomas created a turn-of-the-century theme with pseudo-Tiffany lamps, newsboy caps, and Gay '90s decor. The name, Wendy, came from a real-life, red-haired, freckled girl—Thomas's daughter.

Bob's Big Boy

The late Bob Wian liked to hand out a business card that read, "Robert C. 'Bob' Wian, Fry Cook, retired." A vintage photo shows the young Wian standing at the counter of his first burger stand, wearing a crisp, white fry cook's hat and shirt, an expectant, optimistic expression on his fresh, unlined face. The wall clock says 11:37—just before the lunch rush. The year was 1936. On that first day he'd take in $12—pretty good for the midst of the Great Depression.

Eventually, Thomas sold the franchise back to KFC for $1.5 million and started over again with an innovative concept for a hamburger chain. He planned to serve 100-percent beef burgers, cut square to make better patties, and not placed on the bun until the customer's order was made. To differentiate the atmosphere and emphasize it as an old-fashioned, family-oriented place,

Wian had been working at the Rite Spot restaurant in his hometown of Glendale, California, and seeking to be his own boss. In order to raise capital, he sold his DeSoto

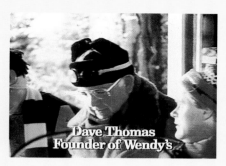

More scenes from the popular Wendy's television spots, featuring Dave Thomas as the ever-exuberant pitchman for his favorite product

roadster for $300 and took a $50 loan from his father. He purchased a 10-stool hamburger stand at 900 Colorado Boulevard in Glendale. The previous owners were two elderly ladies who wanted to get out of the business. Wian renamed the place Bob's Pantry, and it became a popular hangout.

One night in February, 1937, the bass player for a local band didn't order his usual hamburger but asked for "something a little different for a change." This simple request would transform the American hamburger. Wian responded by carving an unsliced sesame bun into three parts, instead of the standard two. Then he spliced in two burger patties and added several layers of cheese, lettuce, and relish. "It looked ridiculous, like a leaning tower," Wian recalled years later. "The double-deck burger juices were absorbed by the center bun. It was delicious, and everybody in the band wanted one." In that epic moment on a cold February night, Bob Wian had created the world's first recorded double-

A young Bob Wian standing at the
counter of his first burger stand

fat-cheeked, overalls-wearing tyke.
Bob's Big Boy was born.

As Jeffrey Tennyson relates in his
book, *Hamburger Heaven,* Wian's
success inspired a battalion of rotund
imitators, whose business names
sounded like a convention of ado-
lescent Jenny Craig clients: Chubby
Boy, Beefy Boy, Brawny Boy, Husky
Boy, Super Boy, Bun Boy, and Fat
Boy, among others.

Wian, who died in 1992, was
among the first to offer employees
health insurance and profit-sharing
plans, and he strove to make restaurant work more professional, rather
than just a transient job. He ultimately sold the Big Boy
chain to

decker hamburger sandwich. The Big
Mac, the Double Whopper, and hundreds of other double-burger sand-
wiches can trace their parentage to
that spontaneous burst of ground-
beef genius.

Demand for this new kind
of burger was huge, and Wian's
business expanded. Inspired by a
chubby 6-year-old boy who lived
down the street, Wian devised the
Big Boy name. A customer who was
a Hollywood cartoonist sketched on
a napkin a picture of a wavy-haired,

Marriott Corp. His varied career included opening a chain of upscale coffee shops, operating a shrimp-processing business, and serving as mayor of Glendale. "There is nothing fantastic in anything I ever did," he said in a 1979 interview. "It was all little things, but it was all for the customer, to let him know we cared."

George Webb

This local chain of "Hamburger Parlors" was established in 1948 on the east side of Milwaukee, at the corner of Ogden and Van Burn streets, by George and Evelyn Webb. Among the Webburgers that have sustained hungry Milwaukeeans for a half-century are the Super George, a double burger with cheese, lettuce, and Thousand Island dressing, and many variations of Cheeseburgers—sensible enough, given that dairy-rich Wisconsin is home of the self-described Cheeseheads. Some Milwaukee residents use the chain's name as a verb, as in, "Want to Webb after work?"

Maureen McLaughlin, a reporter for the *Milwaukee Journal*, wrote that having a burger at George Webb's is like walking into a scene from the movie *Diner:* "Longtime friends sit at their usual table, in their usual seats, and talk—sometimes for six hours at a time—about the typical topics: cars, women, school, the news, and annual trips to Herbster, a little town on Lake Superior."

In 1987 George Webb gave away 168,194 free hamburgers to celebrate the 13-game winning streak of the local baseball team, the Brewers. For reasons that no one can quite remember, every George Webb restaurant has two clocks. There's a vague story about nearby railroad tracks, customers asking what time the train left, and vibrations from the railway knocking clocks off the wall. "That's the story, but there's really no concrete reason why," says Tracy Redlich, a

An early George Webb location. For reasons that no one can quite remember, every George Webb restaurant has two clocks—note the front windows of this location.

copywriter for the chain. "It's all part of the quirky atmosphere."

Fatburger

In the late 1940s, a Los Angeles woman with the melodious name of Lovie Yancey opened a hamburger stand at 3021 South Western Avenue that appealed to the city's musicians. The name "fat" was drawn from the hepcat slang of the era—fat meant you'd really made it, as in Fat City or Fat Cat. Yancey's restaurant featured a jukebox with music that went beyond the Top 40; at Fatburger customers could listen to rhythm and blues, jazz, and classic soul music. Yancey ultimately sold the chain to a New York corporation.

Today, Fatburger is a 32-unit business with headquarters in Santa Monica, California, and revenues of $9 million. In addition to burgers made to order, the chain features fresh-squeezed lemonade and freshly made onion rings, and remains as well-known for its music as its food. "No generic burgers. No lame music," says the company's promotional material. In the *Las Vegas Review-Journal*'s annual "Best of Las Vegas"

The Fatburger promise: "No generic burgers. No lame music."

story, the publication praised the chain: "Fatburger outlets are jukebox noisy, quick on the serve, and the appealing burgers arrive hot and just drippy enough to warrant extra napkins."

Former heavyweight champion George Foreman calls Fatburger's cheeseburgers "The best in the world, no question." Fatburger also received an endorsement of sorts from David Letterman. The comedian's list of "Top Ten Reasons to Visit L.A." stated: "Can get a Fatburger with a happenin' babe."

Carl's Jr. and Hardee's

These two chains now are owned by the same parent, CKE Restaurants Inc., which has headquarters in Anaheim, California. Despite its bland name, CKE is a sort of General Motors of hamburgers, collecting several dif-

ferent nameplates under one corporate roof. The company has a total of nearly 4,000 U.S. restaurants. In addition to Carl's Jr. and Hardee's, CKE also has an ownership interest in hamburger chains Checkers and Rally's, both of which are throwbacks to the drive-through, low-priced format.

Carl N. Karcher, a native of Upper Sandusky, Ohio, quit school after the seventh grade and moved to Orange County, California, to work at his uncle's feed store. While driving a truck to deliver bread to customers, Karcher saw opportunity in the hot dog

stands he supplied. In 1941 he bought a hot-dog cart in Los Angeles for $326 and entered the food service business—his wife, Margaret, operated hot dog cart number two. In 1945 Karcher opened his first full-service restaurant, Carl's Drive-in Barbecue, in Anaheim, introducing the yellow-star logo that still is used. The first Carl's Jr. was opened in 1956 by Karcher and his brother, Donald.

Now 82 years old, Karcher still keeps a hand in the business as chairman emeritus. The chain's recent advertising features the tag line "If it doesn't get all over the place, it doesn't belong in your face," and shows ketchup dripping from burgers in amusing ways, thus endearing the firm to the dry cleaners of America.

Hardee's, which was started by Wilber Hardee in North Carolina in 1960, ultimately grew into the country's fourth-largest hamburger chain. The first Hardee's was a drive-in that sold only hamburgers, french fries, and soft drinks. Over the years the chain absorbed Burger Chef—which once was McDonald's chief rival for national prominence—and Sandy's, a Midwestern hamburger chain. In addition to its hamburger, Hardee's was a pioneer of the fast-food breakfast. Richard Gibson, who covers the restaurant industry for *The Wall Street Journal*, says that "Legions of retirees across small-town U.S.A. bring their morning-coffee mugs to Hardee's to sip and chat."

Chapter Five

LOCAL LEGENDS

The cholesterol police will swoon, but the sensation is Elysian...
— WALL STREET JOURNAL REVIEW OF WINSTEAD'S

ALVIN TRILLIN, THE *NEW Yorker* essayist and food writer, declares that "anybody who doesn't think that the best hamburger place in the world is in his home town is a sissy."

Trillin is right. When it comes to hamburgers, most people are passionate, proud, and partial to a particular place. Those local legends carry on the entrepreneurial tradition of the hamburger's origins. Many of those places are family-owned and operated, with several generations working to sustain and perpetuate the legacy. A few have ex-panded modestly into small chains, but they remain more down-home in spirit than the businesses described in the previous chapter.

Hamburger Companion sought local legends around the United States and tried to identify what distinctive elements made them so special. Contributions came from people who responded to queries posted on Internet forums and discussion groups. In addition, friends and acquaintances formed an ad hoc data-gathering organization, the Land-Based Rapid Mobilization No-Load Pro-Am Cross-Functional

The distinctive art deco spire of Winstead's in Kansas City, Missouri. Its legendary steakburger ranks as one of the best.

Multi-Purpose Fast-Food Research Unit (LBRMNLPACFMPFFRU). They contributed a vast compendium of burger-centric experience, opinions, and knowledge.

We salute a few of those local legends here. In doing so, we pay homage, by proxy, to the thousands of venerable burger restaurants located in cities, hamlets, bus terminals, strip malls, country roads, and highway exit ramps all over America.

Iowa 80 Restaurant

Walcott, Iowa

Located in eastern Iowa, near Davenport, Iowa 80 calls itself "the world's largest truck stop" and attracts 5,000 visitors on a typical day. It's also a favorite road destination for country music performers. In addition to serving 52 tons of beef annually, the facility offers a dentist, a laundry, a movie theater, and a chapel.

The featured burgers at Iowa 80 are called the Little Mama and the Big Mama, 4 and 8 ounces, respectively. Terry Peel, who operates the business with his family, says that the Big Mama is popular with truckers: "It's a two-fisted sandwich, served on a big Kaiser bun. The truckers like it."

The Iowa 80, "the world's largest truck stop," serves over 52 tons of beef annually to visitors from all over the country

The Varsity

Atlanta, Georgia

The Varsity was founded in 1928, and its burgers have drawn generations of students from nearby Georgia Tech, who consume copious amounts of the Varsity's "steaks": Mary Brown steak, hamburger with no bun; Glorified steak, hamburger with mayo, lettuce, and tomato; a Sally Rand steak, a hamburger with nothing on it—ask your grandfather who Sally Rand was; or a good old Steak, hamburger with ketchup, mustard, and pickle. The Varsity says it sells more gallons of another Atlanta institution—Coca-Cola—than does any other single outlet in the world. The drive-in format can accommodate 600 cars and more than 800 people inside; on football days some 30,000 people are served.

The Varsity even offers a guide to the restaurant lingo used by its staff, so the uninitiated can be assured their order is being called correctly by the waiter

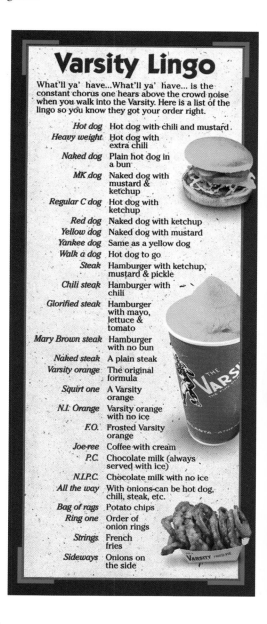

Varsity Lingo

What'll ya' have...What'll ya' have... is the constant chorus one hears above the crowd noise when you walk into the Varsity. Here is a list of the lingo so you know they got your order right.

Hot dog	Hot dog with chili and mustard
Heavy weight	Hot dog with extra chili
Naked dog	Plain hot dog in a bun
MK dog	Naked dog with mustard & ketchup
Regular C dog	Hot dog with ketchup
Red dog	Naked dog with ketchup
Yellow dog	Naked dog with mustard
Yankee dog	Same as a yellow dog
Walk a dog	Hot dog to go
Steak	Hamburger with ketchup, mustard & pickle
Chili steak	Hamburger with chili
Glorified steak	Hamburger with mayo, lettuce & tomato
Mary Brown steak	Hamburger with no bun
Naked steak	A plain steak
Varsity orange	The original formula
Squirt one	A Varsity orange
N.I. Orange	Varsity orange with no ice
F.O.	Frosted Varsity orange
Joe-ree	Coffee with cream
P.C.	Chocolate milk (always served with ice)
N.I.P.C.	Chocolate milk with no ice
All the way	With onions-can be hot dog, chili, steak, etc.
Bag of rags	Potato chips
Ring one	Order of onion rings
Strings	French fries
Sideways	Onions on the side

Cassell's
Tommy's

Los Angeles, California

Southern California has been the birthplace of the drive-through burger, chicken burger, bacon-avocado burger, and the sausage-topped Hockeyburger. In addition to the national chains that were spawned in Southern California are such local legends as Cassell's, which won effusive praise from *Los Angeles* magazine: "The best burger in the city is the one found at the venerable Wilshire District lunchroom Cassell's... a freshly ground softball of USDA prime beef weighing two-thirds of a pound and served naked on a toasted bun. Cassell's hamburgers are the sort you might expect at a quality-obsessed diner somewhere in rural Nebraska, a Spartan, anti-exuberant hamburger qua hamburger in which each element tastes only of itself."

Another L.A. institution is Tommy's, which is famous for its chili burger. Known affectionately to its fans as "Ptomaine Tommy's," the service is walk-up only. The hamburger comes with a fabulously gooey topping of cheese, tomato, and thick chili. Sandy Malloy, an e-mail contributor to the *Hamburger Companion's* research unit, calls Tommy's trademark dish "the sloppiest, messiest, most disgusting, yummiest hamburger in creation (though I don't think I could eat one now). It's popular with college kids from USC, which is nearby, and UCLA, which is across town. When I was in college (at UCLA) I remember going there after a formal dance with a bunch of my sorority sisters and their dates. We had a great time in our gowns and tuxes, chowing down on chili burgers."

Vincenzo's

Louisville, Kentucky

Robin Garr, a food writer, restaurant critic, and stellar member of the LBRMNLPACFMPFFRU, responded to our Internet query and described a once-in-a-lifetime hamburger experience she had while on a writing assignment:

The basic story was a pretty routine local magazine piece, a review of the various burgers around town that included a sampling of McDonald's, local pubs, family restaurants, etc. I gave it a little twist by making it pseudoscientific—I carefully measured each burger and then ranked my reports on the basis of diameter and thickness, ranging from White Castles at one extreme to the locally famous Big Daddy Platter (a 16-ounce burger) at the other.

As a sidebar, I came up with the idea of contacting one of the fanciest restaurants in the city, Vincenzo's, and persuading the host to come up with The Ultimate Hamburger. With a budget of $100, Vincenzo was to create the greatest hamburger the world has ever known.

Vincenzo really got into it: He used a pound of freshly ground prime filet mignon, sautéed to medium-rare in an expensive imported Italian olive oil and then flamed with Louis XIII Cognac and served on a fresh, hot bun specially baked for the occasion from an old family Italian recipe. A selection of mustards and ketchups were served in little baskets carved out of raw vegetables, and the chips were freshly fried Belgian-style pommes frites.

And then, just to provide a proper showcase, Vincenzo surrounded The Burger with Caesar salads prepared at tableside, "just a little dish of pasta" for starters, made with fresh

> *"With a budget of $100, Vincenzo was to create the greatest hamburger the world has ever known."*

swordfish in a Genoese style, and, of course, a selection from the restaurant's justly famous dessert cart.

We chose a red wine with the red meat, a 1981 Tignanello, which at the time was one of the more pricey items on the list, and had a little taste of brandy with the espresso after the meal. The tab ended up right at $200 for two, holding to the budget line of $100 per person and the constant stream of waiters and bussers and sommeliers all through the evening had everybody in the place asking for "Whatever *they're* having."

Vincenzo later told me that after the story appeared, about a dozen people called and asked for the same dinner, and he happily complied— although he did admit that nobody but me got the Louis XIII brandy, which was selling at the time for something like $300 a bottle. Everyone else had their burger flamed with cheaper stuff.

Hudson's
Coeur d'Alene, Idaho

This landmark comes courtesy of Jane and Michael Stern, husband-and-wife authorities on roadside dining and compilers of the "Two for the Road" column in *Gourmet* magazine. The Sterns vividly described the counter scene at Hudson's, an austere Coeur d'Alene institution since 1907 and possibly the only restaurant in Idaho that *doesn't* serve potatoes:

"Pickle or onion?" the counterman will ask when you order a single or double hamburger or cheeseburger…. Your garnish selection is called out to grill man Todd Hudson… who slices the onion to order and uses his knife blade to hoist the thin, crisp disk from the cutting board to the bun bottom; then, deft as a Benihana chef, he cuts eight small circles from a pickle and arrays them in two neat rows atop the onion. Customers enjoy the mesmerizing show from the 17 seats at Hudson's long counter.

When not wielding his knife, Todd swiftly hand-forms each burger, as it is ordered, from a heap of lean ground beef piled in a gleaming silver pan adjacent to his griddle…. There are no side dishes at all: no french fries, no chips, no slaw, not a leaf of lettuce in the house. This is not to say that the staff isn't attuned to the fine points of hamburgerology…. Each patty is cooked until it develops a light crust from the grid-

Glenwood Pines' Pineburger: A 6-ounce cheeseburger served on French bread with lettuce, tomato, onions, and either mayonnaise or Thousand Island dressing

dle but retains a high amount of juiciness inside. One in a bun makes

a balanced sandwich. Two verge on overwhelming beefiness.

Glenwood Pines
Ithaca, New York
White Hut
West Springfield, Massachusetts

Steve Rushmore is president of HVS International, a consulting firm in Mineola, New York, that appraises hotel and resort properties. A constant business traveler, Steve writes an informal newsletter for friends and clients that describes his "road food" finds in unusual and delectable locations.

Rushmore has two hamburger nominations. Glenwood Pines in Ithaca, New York, near the Cornell University campus, wins plaudits for being "the best hamburger in the world. Absolutely the best. It comes on a real good roll.

The burger has a relatively high fat content and is very flavorful."

His second burger site, the White Hut, is "reminiscent of the old White Tower hamburger chain with a 15-seat counter, no written menu, and some of the best-tasting hamburgers in New England," Rushmore says. "The grilled onions are piled 4 inches high on the right side of the grill, and the huge mass of onions simmer for hours, slowly basting themselves in their own juices. Then, at just the right moment, when your hamburger is perfectly cooked, the flipper person scoops up the patty, douses it with a load of hot onions, and places it before you on a paper napkin—no plate."

Red's Java House
Java House

San Francisco, California

If you want a burger and soda where Dashiell Hammett's detective, Sam Spade, might have lunched while tracking down the Maltese Falcon, stop by Red's Java House. It is located near Pier 30 along San Francisco's Embarcadero waterfront—once a hard-boiled, hard-working port district, filled with tattooed stevedores, shady characters, and mysterious ladies. Now it's the gateway to San Francisco's Multimedia Gulch and chock-full of software firms, design houses, and Internet companies. The restaurant was founded as "The Lunchroom" during the early 1930s and was purchased in the 1950s by two brothers, Mike and Tom McGarvey, both of whom had red hair. The current owners are Steve and Maria Reilly.

Red's Java House is a throwback to the trenchcoat-and-fedora era. The humble wood structure still attracts a diverse lunch crowd—construction workers in hard hats sit next to gray-suited bankers and Dockers-clad programmers. A harried-looking, tough-guy grill man, who looks as if he might have tossed down a few shots after hours with Humphrey Bogart, speedily cooks up a tasty burger with onions served on a crunchy roll.

A few blocks south of Red's is a similarly named rival, Java House. It also serves a tasty burger, has great bay views, and is about three ketchup-bottle tosses from San Francisco's new baseball stadium, scheduled to open in May 2000.

Jollibee's

Daly City, California

Jollibee's is the most popular burger chain in the Philippines, outselling McDonald's and capturing half of that country's fast-food market. Its first U.S. outpost, located in a suburb of San Francisco with a large Filipino population, offers burgers with a sweeter, "tomatoey" taste. The Aloha Burger includes a slab of pineapple, and the JolliMeal Champburger has a garlic-and-soy seasoning.

Cotham's

Scott, Arkansas

Praised by a burger fanatic on the Internet, Cotham's is one of two restaurants in the tiny town of Scott. Mary Lee Knoedl, the restaurant's manager, describes its location as "an old, old rundown store building." Its signature dish is the Hubcap Burger, which got its name because it resembles, well, a hubcap, weighing in at one pound and measuring 6 inches in diameter. Children or smaller eaters can get a Lugnut Burger.

Cotham's, on Highway 161 in Scott, Arkansas, is said to be President Bill Clinton's favorite spot for a burger (he loves the signature Hubcap Burger with onion rings)

The Flight Deck
Westfield, Massachusetts

A private pilot named John F. Purner collected hundreds of opinions about burger places in his entertaining book, *The $100 Hamburger: A Guide to Pilots' Favorite Fly-In Restaurants.* "Thousands of contemporary pilots are making burger runs every weekend. I am one of them," Purner writes. "The biggest problem is finding fly-in restaurants.... Pilots simply want to know where they can fly and buy a hamburger, nothing grander than that!" His book is a compilation of burger-eating experiences in or near small airports, contributed by pilots from all over the country.

One of the near-the-runway finds celebrated in Purner's book is The Flight Deck, located at Barnes Municipal Airport in Westfield, Massachusetts: "If you truly desire to taste the wonder of what a $100 hamburger can be like, order the "A-10" and a Coke. Be sure, however, that your plane is not close to its weight limit. Before you depart this fine eatery, be sure to say hello to Effie and the crew."

Another flying burger enthusiast in *The $100 Hamburger* lavishes praise on the Airport Inn at Branch County Airport in Coldwater, Michigan, although, in truth, he was impressed by more than the food: "One day the waitress drove us back to our plane because it was snowing so hard we couldn't see our wingtips from the runway."

Winstead's
Kansas City, Missouri

Kansas City is Calvin Trillin's hometown, and he maintains that Winstead's has the world's best hamburgers (no sissy, he). The business was opened as a drive-in in 1940 by Katherine Winstead and her sister and brother-in-law, Nelle and Gordon Montgomery. The first site, with a distinctive art deco spire, is located near the Nelson-Atkins art gallery; there are 11 other sites around the city. Winstead's calls its hamburgers "steakburgers" and serves them grilled—single, double, or triple—on a plain toasted bun.

A *Wall Street Journal* food writer (and Kansas City native) visited Winstead's in 1998 and lavishly praised both the burgers and the

special thick milk shake, known as a frosty: "Take a bite of steakburger; follow it with a spoonful of frosty, alternating the salty and textured with the sweet and smooth. The cholesterol police will swoon, but the sensation is Elysian…. They do not sell their hamburgers by the billion. You cannot 'supersize' your meal. They

are a household word only in Kansas City. But Calvin Trillin was right: Winstead's has the world's best hamburgers."

'21' Club
New York, New York

Our tour of local legends concludes with this elite restaurant at the vortex of the power lunch. A hamburg-

The hamburger at New York's '21' Club is a favorite among Manhattan's movers and shakers

61

er at '21' is the traditional choice of Manhattan's media moguls, banking barons, and dukes of the deal. The '21' burger costs about $21.40 at lunch and $24 at dinner. "More steak than burger, the '21' comes to table 'nude'—no bun or bread," says Jean Anderson in *The American Century Cookbook: The Most Popular Recipes of the 20th Century*. "[It] is by most accounts the world's best burger. Certainly it's the most expensive."

A well-dressed burger topped with a honey-mustard sauce

Chapter Six

SECRETS OF THE BURGER-MEISTERS

HAT GOES INTO MAKING a great hamburger? *Hamburger Companion* canvassed the authorities on both sides of the hot grill to find out what makes for a classic, memorable, mouth-watering hamburger. We sought opinions about storage, ingredients, heat, grind, toppings—the burger gestalt.

RAW MATERIALS

The consensus of experts is that it all starts with high-quality meat. When we asked Terry Peel of the truck stop Iowa 80 what made a good burger, he responded, "Well, good beef." For Iowa 80, that means pure ground beef, 90-percent lean and 10-percent fat.

Although beef chuck wins the approval of most burger experts, a few recommend ground round or a mixture of chuck with sirloin. Jeffrey Tennyson, author of *Hamburger Heaven*, recommends choice chuck steak with a fat content between 20 and 25 percent. "Ask your butcher to grind it twice—first through a coarse plate and then through a fine one," Tennyson suggests. "The gourmet consensus at

The experts agree: The best ingredients result in the best burger, from the highest quality beef to the freshest in rolls and toppings

this time," says Molly O'Neill, food writer of *The New York Times,* "seems to be ground chuck, with 20-to-25-percent fat content. A grinder, not a food processor, should be used; otherwise the meat would be pulverized."

Bob Cary of Visalia, California, a major franchiser of the A&W Root Beer brand and a former board member of the national A&W Association, views a fat content of about 20 percent as a happy medium. "With 25-to-30-percent fat, you are getting a really juicy and tasty burger, but people these days want to eat a little less fat," says Mr. Cary. "At 15 percent your burger is going to be dry and tougher, with less flavor. Around 20 percent makes your ideal hamburger as far as fat content and flavor."

"Don't let the meat sit in the refrigerator for more than a few hours

afterwards before you cook it," advises Cheryl Alters Jamison and Bill Jamison in their book *Born to Grill.* They also have thoughts on the optimum size of the patty: "Since most buns today are about 3.5 inches across, we usually call for patties

Actor Paul Newman admonishes, "Don't make the mistake of using ground round or sirloin.... Many hamburger chefs fall short of my standards because they use meat that is simply too good."

of that size in recipes, made with approximately 6 ounces of meat.... If a burger is too thick, the outside becomes scorched and dried before the inside cooks adequately. We stay under an inch in thickness, generally about ¾ inch."

Another opinion comes from actor Paul Newman—or at least, it is attributed to Mr. Newman in a press release from Newman's Own, Inc., his specialty food company. In a recipe for a grilled Newmanburger, the actor advises: "Don't make the mistake of using ground round or sirloin in this recipe. Many hamburger chefs fall short of my standards because they use meat that is simply too good. I cook all my hamburgers on the outdoor grill or the indoor fireplace grill, and chuck is best suited to a hot charcoal fire."

Remember these don'ts. As you work with the ground beef in your kitchen, there are several "don't do this" suggestions from the experts:

Don't handle the meat too much. "The less molding and shaping, the more flavorful and juicy the burg-

er," writes Tennyson. "Press the meat just enough to hold the patties together." James Beard, in his book *Simple Foods,* admonishes: "Do not overhandle or press the meat. Too much handling will make the patties heavy and solid, which is not what you want. The meat should just hold together."

Don't be harsh with the patties. The Jamisons write in *Born to Grill,* "Don't compact the beef too tightly in forming patties, and never smash it down with a spatula when you're cooking." "I toss them hand to hand to keep them fluffy," says Paul Newman, perhaps drawing upon the rapid hand motions he learned playing a prizefighter in *Somebody Up There Likes Me.* In a more plaintive tone, Jeffrey Tennyson beseeches us to be gentle with the patties: "Let them sizzle in peace, and be sure to flip them only once." Adds Molly O'Neill, "If you want the burgers to stay juicy, the meat should be handled as little as possible."

Don't undercook the meat. Make sure that the meat cooks thoroughly to eliminate any bacteria that might have entered during preparation and cooking.

DETERMINING DONENESS

Food writers and chefs have numerous descriptions that attempt to identify the perfect point of completion for a burger. Paul Newman aspires to the point at which "a hamburger is crisp on the outside, tomato-red inside." The Jamisons recommend a state of "medium doneness," which they describe as "crusty and richly brown with a bare hint of pink at the center."

James Beard believed in a dual approach, visual and tactile. "When you cut into the hamburger and find it done to your liking, remember how the patty felt when you pressed it. This is a very simple test,

Many burger aficionados warn against compacting a burger too tightly

but it shows you how your fingers can send a message to your brain," Beard wrote.

SIDE DISHES

"Condiments should complement without overwhelming the meat," Tennyson says. "Potato chips and potato salad are standard fare. Grandma might bring jello, and that's okay, too."

The Jamisons are a bit more daring, as they suggest beer-braised onions, guacamole, and mushroom-beer ketchup as attractive side dishes. Yet they also confess, "For a straight-and-narrow stickler, the only proper side dish is a vegetable cooked in oil, either french fries or onion rings, except during the height of the summer season, when fresh corn on the cob joins the acceptable accompaniments." To wash it all down, they continue, "Don't forget the cold cola, drunk directly from the bottle (or even the can) rather than drowned in ice."

Flavorings will vary by region. "There are purists like me," says O'Neill of *The Times*, "who regard anything other than salt and pepper as a heinous crime (a view shared throughout most of the Midwest), while regional lobbies have given rise to chipotle chili pepper burgers (in the Southwest) and marinated burgers (in the Southeast). On either coast, variations on [the] '21' burger—a patty formed around flavored butter—remain very trendy. Among food intelligentsia around the country, homemade ketchup and buns are *de rigeur*."

Look to the classics for inspiration. There's no reason to re-invent the wheel—or the hamburger, for that matter. Television hosts Regis Philbin and Kathie Lee Gifford, in their 1994 book *Entertaining with Regis and Kathie Lee*, revealed the secrets of making a Big Mac at home that "tastes just like the original."

The Trini Burger, another of the gourmet hamburger creations featured in Marcel Desaulniers's book, *The Burger Meisters*

Aided by one of their show's guests, Regis and Kathie Lee deconstructed a Big Mac to determine the precise sequence of the components during assembly. "Build the burger in the following stacking order from the bottom up," they recommend:

1. Bottom bun
2. Half of dressing
3. Half of onion
4. Half of lettuce
5. American cheese
6. Beef patty
7. Middle bun
8. Remainder of dressing
9. Remainder of onion
10. Remainder of lettuce
11. Pickle slices
12. Beef patty
13. Top bun

BE CREATIVE

"You can make the patties round or oval, thick, or fairly flat, according to how you like your hamburger," counseled James Beard. "If you want it rare, make them thick. If you like it medium, make thinner patties.

Chef Marcel Desaulniers,
author of *The Burger Meisters*

Don't worry if they are sort of free-form rather than regular in shape. It's the taste, not the appearance, that matters most."

As mentioned in Chapter One, Marcel Desaulniers of the Trellis

Restaurant, Williamsburg, Virginia, collected recipes and stylings from 47 of America's best chefs into a book called *The Burger Meisters*. Warning: Reading this book will make you hungry. If you aren't tempted by the Wisconsin Camp-Fire Burger, the Trini burger, the Sicilian burger, or the Missouri Sirloin and Blue Cheese Burger, then you will be enticed by the West Indies Burger, with Mango Chutney and Fried Plantains. Chef Desaulniers provides further advice:

When it comes to burgers, there are so many variables that only personal experience seems to confirm the best method. So be brave and experiment. Just don't be foolish and get the fire too hot (I did just that on opening of The Trellis in November 1980, setting off a fire suppressant system and almost canceling the opening festivities!).

Marcel Desaulniers advises burger fanciers to "be brave and experiment."

Chapter Seven

BURGERS AND BILLIONAIRES

HE TWO WEALTHIEST persons in America, Bill Gates and Warren Buffett, are both passionate fans of the hamburger. Not only do these gentlemen know how to calculate profitability and build shareholder value, they shrewdly appreciate the intrinsic value of a good burger.

Gates, the co-founder and chief executive of Microsoft, integrated hamburgers into the corporate culture early on. Stephen Manes and Paul Andrews write in their 1993 Gates biography that, shortly after hiring its 100th employee in No-

vember 1981, Microsoft moved into a two-story office building in Bellevue, Washington:

The move continued several Microsoft traditions and started a new one: dining at Burgermaster, the drive-in restaurant right next door, whose cheeseburgers and shakes quickly became a long-standing Bill Gates lunch ritual.

By April Burgermaster had become such an essential aspect of Microsoft that a path had been cut between it and the offices, and it had acquired the "speed dialing"

Cheeseburgers and shakes at Burgermaster, the drive-in restaurant next door to Microsoft's Bellevue, Washington, office building, became a long-standing Bill Gates lunch ritual

number of 611 on the Microsoft phone system.

Even when Microsoft became a powerful, publicly traded corporation, the burger affinity survived. To paraphrase the computer jargon, Gates is burger-friendly. In 1994 *Forbes ASAP* editor Rich Karlgaard accompanied Gates on a road trip and kept a diary of Gates's activities, which included continual hamburger breaks:

> Gates is offered a box lunch and seems uninterested, but when told it is a cheeseburger his eyes light up: "A cheeseburger! I am *seduced!*… [Several days later] For lunch Bill comforts himself with yet another cheeseburger, this one the $16.95 hotel variety.… [Waiting in an airport lounge for a delayed flight] Gates eases the pain with a greasy cheeseburger and fries from a nearby food stall.

Returning from a trip to China in 1995, Gates and his entourage found themselves in Hong Kong after midnight: "We were really happy to discover that they have a 24-hour McDonald's in Hong Kong," he told an Asian journalist, who added that Gates "wolfed down hamburgers."

It is evident that if Gates hadn't gone into computers, he would have rivaled Ray Kroc in his unrelenting passion for, and all-consuming commitment to, hamburgers.

Similarly, Warren Buffett has a well-documented affection for burgers. Roger Lowenstein of *The Wall Street Journal*, in a 1995 biography of Buffett, describes how Buffett and his wife joined a gourmet cooking club, in which couples took turns preparing Swedish meatballs and French crêpes. "Each time, though, Warren would pleasantly ask the hostess to make him a hamburger," Lowenstein writes.

When Buffett contemplates his next billion-dollar investment in his Omaha office, "He often lunches alone, sending out for a cheeseburger and french fries." Lowenstein describes what happened when Buffett visited Katharine Graham, the regal owner of the *Washington Post* news-

cheeseburgers and fried—what do you call them?—french fries, all drowned in salt."

Katherine Graham, owner of the *Washington Post,* graciously accommodated shareholder Warren Buffett's predilection for cheeseburgers during one of his visits to her home for dinner

paper, in which Buffett is a major shareholder:

Katherine Graham told her cook to make hamburgers when Buffett was in town. "When he arrived," she said with reflexive snobbery, "it was only

In the 1997 annual report of his company, Berkshire Hathaway, Buffett uses the hamburgers to teach a lesson about the stock market:

A short quiz: If you plan to eat hamburgers throughout your life and are not a cattle producer, should you wish for higher or lower prices for beef?... Many investors get this wrong. Even though they are going

Hamburgers are mentioned by Lee Iacocca, the automobile executive whose comeback saga—fired by Henry Ford, leader of a resurgence

Lee Iacocca discovered the secret behind the hamburgers at the Ford executive dining room, the only place Henry Ford claimed you could get a decent burger

to be net buyers of stocks for many years to come, they are elated when stock prices rise and depressed when they fall. In effect, they rejoice because prices have risen for "hamburgers" they will soon be buying. This reaction makes no sense.

at Chrysler —was an inspirational best-seller in the 1980s. Iacocca relates this anecdote about Ford's executive dining room:

You could order anything you wanted in that room, from oysters Rockefeller to roast pheasant. But Henry's standard meal was a hamburger. He rarely ate anything else. One day at lunch he turned to me and complained that his personal chef at home, who was earning something like $30,000 or $40,000 a year, couldn't even make a decent hamburger. Furthermore, no restaurant he had ever been to could make a hamburger the way he liked it—the way it was prepared for him in the executive dining room.

I like to cook, so I was fascinated by Henry's complaint. I went into the kitchen to speak to Joe Bernardi, our Swiss-Italian chef. "Joe," I said,

"Henry really likes the way you make hamburger. Could you show me how?"

"Sure," said Joe. "But you have to be a great chef to do it right so watch me very carefully."

He went over to the fridge, took out an inch-thick New York strip steak, and dropped in into the grinder. Out came the ground meat, which Joe fashioned into a hamburger patty. Then he slapped it onto the grill.

"Any questions?" he asked.

Then he looked up with a half smile and said: "Amazing what you can cook up when you start with a five-dollar hunk of meat!"

Chapter Eight

POP GOES THE BURGER

$\mathcal{T}$HE HAMBURGER IS SO intertwined with popular culture that it's impossible to determine which one has a greater impact on the other. The sweep of the hamburger encompasses movies, music, cartoons, advertising, slang, and even politics. Here are some snapshots of the burger in American pop life:

A HUNKA, HUNKA BURNING BURGER

Elvis Presley's taste in burgers wasn't of the "Love Me Tender" variety.

Instead, the King liked his burgers "burned to a crisp. He often sent his back until it was what some people would call totally charred," says food writer Irena Chalmers in *The Great Food Almanac.* After his death, Elvis continued to enjoy burgers by patronizing a Burger King in Kalamazoo, Michigan.

LYRICS OF DESIRE AND LONELINESS

Jimmy Buffett, the songwriter best known for celebrating life in "Margaritaville," has a tune called

Charcoal King: Elvis loved a good burger, but only if it was "burned to a crisp."

"Cheeseburger in Paradise," which describes his attempt to adhere to a health food diet: "Tried to amend my carnivorous habits, made it nearly 60 days/Drinkin' lots of carrot juice and soakin' up rays/But at night I have these wonderful dreams, some kind

"Somebody give me a cheeseburger!" in the song "Livin' in the USA."

A different sentiment comes from Hank Williams, Jr., whose song "Something to Believe In" concerns a country boy who moves to Los Angeles and battles the big city's

Jimmy Buffett,
"Cheeseburger in Paradise":
"But at night I have these wonderful dreams, some kind of carnivorous treat."

of carnivorous treat." In a similar vein, The Steve Miller Band pleaded,

loneliness: "I was out walkin' down the street/ When I met a girl/by the

Burger World/and I was needin' her company."

TWO´S COMPANY

In one of those epic moments of cultural karma, Ray Kroc of Mc-

World War I, both young Midwesterners served in a volunteer ambulance corps in France. Kroc would later recall that "He [Disney] was always drawing pictures while the rest of us were chasing girls." Late in his career, Kroc toyed

Cultural karma: Ray Kroc, McDonald's CEO, and Walt Disney served together in France during World War I

Donald's and Walt Disney knew each other as young men. During

with the idea of opening a McDonald's amusement park that would

compete directly against Disney-land, but he was talked out of it by McDonald's board members.

WHERE'S THE BEEF?

On the night of January 9, 1984, a Wendy's television commercial made its national debut. The commercial showed three elderly ladies examining a giant hamburger bun. The bun was removed, revealing a pathetically small hamburger. One of the women, a former manicurist from Illinois named Clara Peller, uttered the line, "Where's the beef?"

The ad was a sensation and inspired three sequels based on the same slogan. The late Mrs. Peller became a media celebrity, Wendy's sales increased by 36 percent, and the expression "Where's the beef?" became a slang expression and the punch-line for hundreds of off-color jokes.

"Where's the beef?" The Wendy's commercial turned Clara Peller into a media celebrity and increased sales by 36 percent.

The stakes got even higher when two rivals for the 1984 Democratic presidential nomination, Walter Mondale and Gary Hart, appeared on a television debate. Mondale skewered his opponent, who claimed to be the candidate of new ideas, by turning to Hart and asking, in his Minnesota twang, "Where's the beef?"

Amazingly, the commercial's appeal has endured the rapid shifts of pop culture. A market research firm conducted a survey in 1998 to see which television commercials were popular among teenagers. Irma Zandl, the firm's president, found that 18- and 19-year-olds considered Clara Peller's "Where the beef" commercials their favorite—"and they were tiny, tiny tots at the time the commercials ran."

KITSCH AND A HARLEY

A ceramic bank. A salt-and-pepper set. A transistor radio. A paper-weight, a lamp, a wrist-watch, a telephone—all these and more, lovingly molded in the image of a hamburger. Many of these kitsch objects are displayed in Jeffrey Tennyson's book

timable position by producing its likeness and form in an infinite variety of objects and artifacts. This tribute to good taste—the visual manifestation

Some of the hamburger kitsch on display at the Hamburger Hall of Fame in Seymour, Wisconsin

Hamburger Heaven. Tennyson, a photographer and graphic designer, writes:

It is a testimony to the hamburger that we have seen fit to acknowledge its es-

of hamburger appreciation—illuminates the burger as an important sociocultural icon and institution.

For those seeking a first-hand experience with hamburgeriana, there's the International Hamburger Hall of Fame in Daytona Beach, Florida. Harry Sperl maintains the museum in a room of his house. His 500-plus objects that are shaped like hamburgers include biscuit jars, clocks, hats, trays, erasers, badges, music boxes, and a water bed, which has a sesame-seed-covered spread and matching pillows. The pinnacle of Sperl's collection is the "Hamburger Trike"—a Harley-Davidson motorcycle on which is mounted a huge hamburger carved out of Styrofoam and complete with depictions of cheese, pickles, onions, lettuce, tomato, and ketchup bottles. A stereo on the Trike plays the sound of frying hamburgers.

WIMPY

When the cartoon strip "Thimble Theatre" by artist E.C. Segar debuted in 1919, its cast included Pop-

eye, Olive Oyl, Sweet Pea, Bluto, and J. Wellington Wimpy, a derby-hatted, neck-tied, smiling gentleman. Popeye's current syndicator, King Features, describes Wimpy as "the world's most hamburger-obsessed moocher.... His catch phrase, 'I'll gladly pay you Tuesday for a hamburger today,' has made him

Wimpy: "I'll gladly pay you Tuesday for a hamburger today..."

one of the many popular supporting characters to come out of this strip."

Actor Paul Dooley portrayed Wimpy in the 1980 *Popeye* movie, which cast Robin Williams in the title role. A chain called Wimpy's Grills began in Bloomington, Indiana, in 1934 and went out of business in the U.S. following its founder's death in 1978. A Wimpy's hamburger chain still does business in Europe.

JUGHEAD

Another burger aficionado from the cartoon world is Jughead, the laid-back high school chum in the "Archie" comic books. In a 1970 drawing, Archie and Jughead are seen in a fine-arts museum, admiring the sculpture "Burger" by "Dandy Warhog." Archie exclaims, "Jughead, this burger is a work of art." In response, Jughead—who is munching on a hamburger—cooly states, "Archie, *every* burger is a work of art!"

HAPPY NEW BURGER

For 27 years Dick Clark has been the man Americans watch on television from Times Square, New York, on New Year's Eve. But what does Clark do after the ball drops? What is his first meal of the first day of January? "After New Year's," he told a reporter, "it's become a ritual for me to go to P.J. Clarke's, go to the back room, and have a hamburger and a beer with my wife."

REALLY BIG CUCUMBERS

The hamburger's popularity has influenced other aspects of the food industry. In October 1998, Vlasic Foods introduced Hamburger Stackers—extremely large pickle chips intended to cover an entire hamburger. The product was developed in response to consumers' complaints that they were having a hard time keeping the pickles from falling off the burgers.

Vlasic said the new product, which is expected to generate at least

$20 million in sales, would use jumbo cucumbers more than 10 times larger than the standard pickle cucumber (known as the 3A). The new Vlasic pickle derives from a hybrid cucumber that is derived from a variety known as 5B, which is used in Europe. "These are palpably exciting times at Vlasic," reported *The Wall Street Journal.*

MODEL BEHAVIOR

According to the fashion magazine *Allure,* eating hamburgers is chic

Naomi Campbell: master of the art of chowing down and still looking good

among many supermodels: "Probably the ultimate expression of macho eating is chowing down and still looking good. 'Naomi [Campbell] I've seen on the beach in 100-degree weather eating ribs, onion rings, a hamburger, french fries, Tabasco sauce, everything,' marvels one fashion insider. 'And Bridget Hall, no matter what, has to have McDonald's number five with mayonnaise.'"

In an attempt to keep morale high during Operation Desert Shield and Desert Storm, great emphasis was placed on providing tempting food for the soldiers. Suppliers were found who could get fresh, familiar foods to the troops instead of the traditional military rations.

WARRIOR BURGERS

Lt. General William "Gus" Pagonis was in charge of logistics for Operation Desert Shield and Desert Storm in 1990-91. In his book *Moving Mountains,* Pagonis describes the emphasis that he placed on tempting food for the soldiers. He worked with a senior warrant officer, Wesley Wolf, to find suppliers who could get fresh, familiar foods to the troops instead of the traditional military rations. One of these foods was a "Wolfburger"—named after Wes Wolf—which was delivered from specially designed vehicles known as Wolfmobiles:

Imagine that you've been at some remote and desolate desert site for weeks, or even months, consuming dehydrated or vacuum-packed military rations. One day, unannounced, an odd-looking vehicle with the word Wolfmobile painted on it comes driving into your camp. The side panels open up, and a smiling crew inside offer to cook you a hamburger to order. "Side of fries? How about a Coke?"

"There's no doubt in my mind that these developments had a direct impact on the success of the war."

"There's no doubt in my mind that these developments had a direct impact on the success of the war," Pagonis says.

Y2K BURGER

A joke letter on the Internet in November 1998 warned that McDonald's would suffer its own version of the Year 2000 computer melt-down. According to the spoof, which was described in *The Wall Street Journal*, the neon signs that boast of 99 billion burgers sold (or 99 Gigaburgers) will be unable to roll over to 100

"Billions and Billions Sold," without getting into precise statistics. The company estimates that it passed the 99 billion mark in 1994.

The New York Yankees' Joe Torre, who proves that hot dogs are not the only province of baseball

AN APPETITE FOR THE GAME

Baseball is usually associated with hot dogs, but hamburgers figured in an anecdote from Joe Torre, former infielder and current manager of the New York Yankees: "I remember years ago in San Diego, I had made two errors on two plays. I was playing third base and somebody kept calling me a hamburger out there, and by about the third error, I was starting to get hungry."

Gigaburgers. The signs will misfire and display only '00 Billion Burgers Sold, causing consumers to lose confidence in the company and injuring the economy.

In reality, most McDonald's restaurants have signs that simply say

BIG SCREEN, SMALL SCREEN

Many linkages exist between hamburgers and the worlds of movies and television. Both flourished in the moderate weather and automobile culture of Southern California. Bing Crosby played a hamburger mogul named Howard Harvey in the 1960 movie *High Time,* and burger parlors have served as back-

A running skit on television's original *Saturday Night Live* depicted the mythical Olympia Diner, in which the owner (John Belushi) and the cook (Dan Aykroyd) evoked typhoons of laughter by shouting, "chee'burger, chee'burger." On the

drops for innumerable movie scenes. George Lucas used the classic burger drive-in as the centerpiece for *American Graffiti.*

TV show *Happy Days,* the character Fonzie was usually at Al's Diner, eating a hamburger and dispensing the wisdom of the streets.

Quentin Tarantino, one of the most prominent of the new Hollywood directors, frequently uses hamburgers as a touchstone. In Tarantino's *Pulp Fiction* (1994), Vincent Vega (John Travolta) and Jules (Samuel L. Jackson) have an extensive and expletive-laden debate about how the French refer to Big Macs and Whoppers.

In another contemporary movie, *Reality Bites* (1994), the character Troy Dyer (Ethan Hawke) offers deep philosophical insights:

There's no point to any of this. It's all just a… a random lottery of meaningless tragedy and a series of near escapes. So I take pleasure in the details. You know… a quarter-pounder with cheese, those are good…

THE ASIAN BURGER

Yunxiang Yan, an anthropologist at UCLA, describes the impact of McDonald's in mainland China:

"Eating at McDonald's has become a meaningful social event for Beijing residents…. A considerable proportion of customers were tourists from outlying provinces who had only heard about McDonald's or seen its Golden Arches in the movies. Tasting American food recently has become an important aspect of Chinese tourism in Beijing, and those who achieve this goal boast about it to their relatives and friends back home."

Harvard professor James L. Watson, who edited a collection of essays, *Golden Arches East: McDonald's in East Asia,* relates this anecdote:

When the son of a Japanese executive first spotted the Golden Arches while traveling with his family in North America, he exclaimed, "They even have McDonald's in the United States!"

Professor Yan, the UCLA anthropologist, described this experience with a group of Chinese schoolchildren:

I discovered that Ronald McDonald is a very popular figure among children. Not one of the 68 youngsters (from the third to sixth grade) I spoke with failed to recognize the image of Ronald McDonald; most students appeared very excited when I asked about him. All the children said they liked Ronald because he was funny, gentle, kind, and he understood children's hearts. About one-third believed that Ronald McDonald came from America; the majority insisted that he came from the McDonald's headquarters in Beijing. When I asked these children to tell me the most interesting experience they had had at McDonald's, a sixth grader said it was the time he went to McDonald's with four friends to celebrate his birthday, unaccompanied by adults. They made a reservation so that

Aunt McDonald had prepared a table for them in advance and helped them recite poems, sing songs, and play games. A third-grader said she was very happy when she heard her own name announced over the loudspeakers at McDonald's, accompanied by "Happy birthday to you."

When I was about to leave after finishing my group interview, a third-grade boy came up to me and asked: "Are you Uncle McDonald?"

"No, I'm not."

"You have his eyes."

Assuming a serious demeanor, the boy then showed me a pen with a small hamburger on it—a gift he received from Ronald McDonald. It became clear to me that for this little boy and many of his friends, Uncle McDonald is real, and he is also an important influence on these children's lives.

麥當勞叔叔生日會，
又熱鬧、又方便；媽咪放心，大家開心！
詳情請向本餐廳經理查詢。

**Ronald McDonald Birthday Parties
are Funtastic! They're great for Moms too!**
Ask us about planning *your* next Ronald McDonald Birthday Party.

Chapter Nine

THE RAW AND
THE COOKED

HERE'S A PARTICULAR kind of mood that results when people get together to enjoy themselves over food and beverages. The Irish call it *craic*—pronounced "crack"—which roughly translates as the spontaneous good spirits that fill a pub. Stuart Emmrich, a writer for *Smart Money,* described his experience in Dublin:

I'm sitting in a pub in downtown Dublin, nestled in a corner booth, a book in one hand, a pint of Guinness in the other. An excellent Irish band is playing on a stage about 15 feet away, and a warm fire is going about 10 feet to my left.... Some of the pubs, particularly those with live music, often play host to entire families—the parents knocking back a pint or two while the kids gather at the foot of the stage, matching their steps to those of a small group of Irish dancers.... The family scene is especially strong on Sunday afternoons, when the traditional pubs serve a "carvery lunch" to their patrons.

In the United States, the hamburger restaurant—often referred to with

The hamburger cuts across social, occupational, and ethnic boundaries, which also makes it a good fit with America

gruff affection as "the joint"—is where we go for communal friendship and food. Our culture is ambivalent about alcohol, and we have never adapted the European attitude, in which a pub serving alcoholic beverages is an inviting and comfortable place for men and women, grandparents and children (and pets, too). Yet almost everyone in the U.S. eats hamburgers, and those few who don't happily will munch the french fries. The hamburger joint, in short, is the American pub.

Americans need a place to go, and the hamburger provides the

Winstead's, in Kansas City, Missouri, is representative of the ideal American "burger joint"— an inviting place to go for communal friendship and food

place. Tom Miller, a third-generation Kansas City resident, told *The Wall Street Journal* in 1998 about his fondness for Winstead's, a local hamburger chain:

[In the 1940s] we went on good-time dates—a group of us would go to a movie and sit in the cheaper seats. Then we'd head over to Winstead's and get a steakburger and a frosty. It was "see and be seen." People would go from car to car and visit, and then everybody would pull out with a grand squeal of tires. During the war, if you were lucky enough to get a furlough, the first you did was head for Winstead's.

Connie Llamas, a carhop at Winstead's for 25 years, agrees. "People who retired and moved away come back on vacations—they think Winstead's is the place to be. And it is."

At the same time, Americans aren't much for lingering over food. We are not a chatty people (with the exception of talk-radio sports programs). Meals are arranged as much for efficiency as for gustatory pleas-

ure or camaraderie. We're very busy being busy, or at least maintaining the appearance of being busy.

There's nothing much new about this. A British visitor in the 1820s complained that Americans "ate with the greatest possible rapidity," and a Japanese writer, visiting Chicago around 1900, described America as "the place where people grab food and eat while standing."

Hamburgers are a perfect compromise between our desire for community and our compulsion to get going. A hamburger cooks quickly and can be eaten quickly. If you want to eat it while driving, you take it back in the car and devour it with one hand. It is just filling enough to satiate hunger without dulling your energy or making you feel bloated.

It is a tribute to the American genius that we've taken the neighborhood pub, converted it into a hamburger joint and distributed it everywhere, so that wherever we go—there it is. The late Charles Kuralt, who reported from the road for many years on CBS, described the ubiquity of the burger:

You can find your way across this country using burger joints the way a navigator uses stars.... We have

had a Capitol burger—guess where. And so help us, in the inner courtyard of the Pentagon, a Penta burger... and then there was the night in New Mexico when a lady was just closing up, and we had to decide in a hurry. What'll it be, she said, a

munched Bridge burgers in the shadow of the Brooklyn Bridge and Cable burgers hard by the Golden Gate, Dixie burgers in the sunny South and Yankee Doodle burgers in the North. The Civil War must be over—they taste exactly alike.... We

whoppa burger or a bitta burger? Hard to decide....

But this is not merely a local phenomenon. The smell of fried onions is abroad in the land, and if the French chefs among us avert their eyes, we will finish reciting our menu of the last few weeks on the highways of America. We've had grabba burgers, kinga burgers, lotta burgers, castle burgers, country burgers, bronco burgers, Broadway burgers, broiled burgers, beefnut burgers, bell burgers, plush burgers, prime burgers, flame burgers... dude burgers, char burgers, tall boy burgers, golden burgers, 747 jet burgers, whiz burgers, nifty burgers, and thing burgers.

Now the hamburger place is the vehicle for bringing this American attribute to other cultures. Yunxiang Yan, the UCLA anthropologist quoted in the previous chapter, described a McDonald's in Beijing:

I once observed two people seated in a McDonald's restaurant for over two hours, discussing handbag sales.... young couples and teenagers are particularly fond of frequenting McDonald's because they consider the environment romantic. Women in all age groups tend to spend the

longest time in McDonald's, irrespective of whether they are alone or with friends.... Similar views appear to be common among older people.... It has become a routine for [retired people] to order a hamburger and a drink and then chat for one or two hours—sometimes even longer. They told me that they liked the setting: It is clean, bright, and air-conditioned, better than their memories of Beijing's old-style teahouses.

When I asked if there were other regular older customers like themselves, they said "of course," and, smiling, told me they had made new friends at McDonald's.

A similar phenomenon is happening in Taiwan, according to David Y. H. Wu, an anthropologist from Hong Kong's Chinese University:

Single individuals often treat McDonald's as a place to read, think, or simply kill time—often for over an hour at a sitting. I observed many older people who ordered a cup of tea and sat, quietly by themselves, for an entire morning. Business people frequently arrived with briefcases and used the restaurant for meetings lasting for over an hour. Young people treated McDonald's as a meeting place and a convenient setting for courtship. In no instance did I observe McDonald's staff trying to eject any of the customers; nor were efforts made to make lingerers feel uncomfortable. It is clear that from the local perspective, McDonald's is a public space, much like a park or library....

The hamburger cuts across social, occupational, and ethnic boundaries, which also makes it a good fit with America. Marcel Desaulniers, the distinguished chef-proprietor of the Trellis Restaurant, writes: "Burgers are the favorite food of the hard hat on the construction project, the busy nurse on an all-night shift, the movie star on location, the executive after a few days in almost any foreign venue, and, most certainly, the professional chef."

JoAnn di Lorenzo, owner of JoAnn's Cafe in South San Francisco, California, calls hamburgers "a populist food. They do exactly what they are supposed to do; they're straightforward, and they're not foo-foo. Hamburgers fill your belly, they smell good and taste good. Americans are an anti-monarch society—we loved Princess Diana more than Queen Elizabeth, because Diana seemed so normal and down-to-earth. It's the same with the hamburger—it's really popular because it's people food."

That's why hamburgers are a source of consolation and support during troubled times. All of us rely on food while coping with pain, grief, or despair, and the foods we crave are the old reliables, the standards, the familiar tastes and textures.

Consider the experience of George Foreman. After losing the world heavyweight title to Muhammad Ali in 1974 (the fight depicted in the documentary film *When They Were Kings*), Foreman fell into a devastating depression. He ultimately recovered, made a lucrative comeback in boxing, and launched a successful second career as an affable entertainer and blithe corporate spokesman. He told a sportswriter from the *Los Angeles Times* how he recovered from depression:

I looked around at what boxing had given me, all the cars, the houses, and all the money, and I was depressed because it seemed like there was something else I should be happy about, but I couldn't figure

out what it was. Well, it was cheeseburgers. One day, I drove down to a Jack in the Box near where I lived then, drove through in my Rolls-Royce, and bought a burger.

I drove home and ate it, and it hit me. I suddenly remembered what I'd dreamed of that day, when I left Houston, the ability to buy all the burgers I wanted. When you walk around hungry, food is important. And you never forget. So I went right back to that Jack in the Box and bought another one.

Wheat bran and Vitamin B-12 tablets might make you feel good, but when you get ready to fight and you tell your body, "O.K. body, let's go," nothing happens. But I eat a cheeseburger and, *ta-da,* I'm ready to fight.

Kids' Burger Taste Testing

IT SEEMED SO EASY. Market research firms get big bucks for putting a bunch of kids around a table, feeding them hamburgers, and recording their preferences and pithy remarks. Nothing to it.

In that spirit, *The Hamburger Companion* invited every kid we knew, and their parents, to join us for a Saturday afternoon taste test. A hamburger procurement team fanned out over a middle-class suburban region at 11 A.M. to gather burgers anonymously from four well-known chains (heretofore to be cleverly referred as Burger #1, Burger #2, Burger #3, and Burger #4).

A little after noon, the nine children, ranging in age from 3 to 12, assembled in the kitchen and took their seats at the testing table. The mood was brisk, professional. The children sampled the burgers one brand at a time, pausing only to cleanse their palates with cold water and to visit the bathroom. Par-

cisms. Burger brand bashing was fierce. The verbal abuse hurled at the burgers was extreme, and was no less severe for the buns and condiments.

However, the kids also *ate* all of the hamburgers with gusto and went back for seconds. We did notice a follow-the-leader pattern: As soon as one youngster made a negative comment, everyone else jumped in, making even more derogatory remarks, until the taste test seemed like a children's version of *Can You Top This?* combined with *The Gong Show*.

After 30 minutes and four rounds of judicious, discriminating taste testing,

ents were barred from sitting at the table, but were permitted to stand by in the kitchen and "help out" by eating surplus burgers. The kids were asked to make a crayon drawing after each serving, and to express their innermost emotions, preferences, and musings on hamburgers.

Results? Inconclusive. The kids complained about *all* of the hamburgers. In fact, they were merciless in their criti-

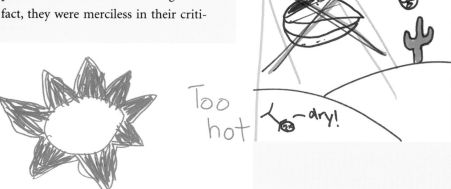

the panel members declared themselves full of hamburgers. It also was evident, based on the degree of squirming, restless pounding on the table, talking to their neighbors, and appeals made to Mommy, that the panel had had quite enough. The taste test took adjournment, and the panelists regrouped in the den to watch *Honey, I Shrunk the Kids, The TV Show*—which, strangely enough, concerned the adventures of two miniaturized men who were lost inside a hamburger stand.

Here's a sampling of the comments. *The Hamburger Companion's* main conclusion: vast relief that we aren't in the business of food research with children.

BURGER #1
Fiona: It's too hot.
Jackie: Too greasy.
Kyle: No.
Nathan: That's hot!
Steve: I don't like the onions.

BURGER #2
Steve: Too dry.
Justine: The meat is a little dry. It looks like a desert to me.
Jackie: Too much ketchup.
Kyle: I don't like it.
Gregory: It's bad.

BURGER #3
Justine: Too much mustard.
Heather: Take off the onions.
Nathan: I like it.
Scott: The bread is sticky.
Jackie: Too dry.

BURGER #4
Scott: I don't want it.
Gregory: It doesn't have very much taste.
Jackie: I don't like it.
Justine: (motioning) Thumbs down.
Fiona: (drawing) A hamburger is a circle.

ACKNOWLEDGMENTS

Hamburger Companion is grateful to those who served as stalwart guides on our hamburger expedition. We have a special debt to a few people who were particularly informative and generous with their time and knowledge:

Adrian Bonnar, Bistro Burger, San Francisco

JoAnn diLorenzo, JoAnn's Cafe, South San Francisco, California

Steve Rushmore, HVS International, Mineola, New York

Barbara Pisani and Christi Nelson, Lebhar-Friedman, New York, researchers for the *Companion* series

Beth G. Klein, librarian, California Culinary Academy, San Francisco

Craig Jackson and Lucinda Walker, reference specialists, Mechanics' Institute Library, San Francisco

The children and parents who participated in our hamburger tasting

The National Cattlemen's Beef Association

Marcel Desaulnier, Trellis Restaurant, Williamsburg, Virginia

Geoff Golson and Paul Frumkin at Lebhar-Friedman Books, New York, who had the original vision and enthusiasm for the *Companion* series.

PHOTO CREDITS

Bob's Big Boy: pages 42, 43

Burger King: page 35: Burger King® trademarks, trade name and photographs are reproduced with permission from Burger King Corporation

Checkers/Rally's Restaurants Inc.: page 47

Corbis: page 27

Corbis/AFP: page 92

Corbis/Alissa Crandall: page 97

Corbis/Bettmann: pages 21, 24, 27, 80, 84

Corbis/Judy Griesedieck: page 74

Corbis/Wally McNamee: page 78

Corbis/Matthew Mendelsohn: page 77

Corbis/Neal Preston: page 82

Corbis/Peter Turnley: page 3

Corbis/Photo B.D.V.: page 89

Cotham's Restaurant: page 59

Fatburger Corporation: page 46

George Webb Restaurants: page 45

Glenwood Pines: page 57

Dennis Gottlieb: front cover, ii

Michael Grand: pages vi, 68, 70, 72, 73

David Graulich: pages 106, 107

Home of the Hamburger: pages 23, 86

Iowa 80 Restaurant Ltd.: page 52

Jack in the Box: page 12

©1993 King Features Syndicate Inc.: page 87

McDonald's Corporation: pages 33, 83

National Cattlemen's Beef Association: pages x, 13, 17, 49, 63, 95, 98, 102, 109

Nation's Restaurant News: pages 37, 43, 90

Newman's Own Inc.: page 66

©1999 PhotoDisc Inc.: pages 6, 9, 10, 64, 93

Charles E. Rotkin/©Corbis: page 18

'21' Club: page 61

The Varsity, page 53

Wendy's International Inc.: pages 38, 40, 41

©1998 White Castle System Inc./All rights reserved: pages 28, 30

Winstead's® & Waid's Co.: pages 50, 100

INDEX

Airport Inn (Coldwater, Michigan), 60
Ali, Muhammad, 105
American Graffiti (movie), 93
Anderson, Jean, 62
Anderson, Walter, 26–28
Andrews, Paul, 75
Asia, 8, 59, 76, 94–96, 103–4
automobiles, 25–26, 35–36, 101
A&W Root Beer, 66

baseball, 44, 92
Beard, James, 67, 69, 71–72
Berkshire Hathaway, 77–78
Bernardi, Joe, 79
Bistro Burger (San Francisco), 4–5
Bob's Big Boy, 40–44
Bonnar, Adrian, 4–5
Buffett, Jimmy, 81–82
Buffett, Warren, 75, 76–78
buns, hamburger, 2, 26, 52, 71
Burger Chef, 48
Burger King
    Double Whopper, 42–43
    founding of, 34–37
    Whopper, 35–36

Campbell, Naomi, 89, 90
Carl's Jr., 47–48
Cary, Bob, 66
Cassell's (Los Angeles), 54
Chalmers, Irena, 81
Checkers, 47
cheeseburgers, 6, 12, 13, 15, 42, 44, 47, 54, 76–77
children
    burger taste test, 106–8
    in China, 94–96
chili burgers, 54
China, People's Republic of, 94–96, 103
CKE Restaurants, Inc., 47–48
Clark, Dick, 88

Clinton, Bill, 59
Coca-Cola, 53
college students, 7–8, 53, 54, 57–58
corn on the cob, 69
Cotham's (Scott, Arkansas), 59

Davis, Fletcher ("Old Dave"), 25
Delmonico's Restaurant (New York City), 22
Desaulniers, Marcel, 5, 70, 72, 104
diLorenzo, JoAnn, 104
Diner (movie), 44
Disney, Walt, 83–85
double-deck burger, 42–43

Economist, The, 2–4, 12–13
Edgerton, David, 34–37
Emmrich, Stuart, 99

Fatburger, 45–47
Fisher, M. F. K., 6–7
The Flight Deck (Westfield, Massachusetts), 60
Florida, 86–87
Ford, Henry, 78–79
Foreman, George, 47, 105
french fries, 2, 31, 34, 48, 69, 100

Garr, Robin, 54–56
Gates, Bill, 74, 75–76
General Mills, 15–16
Genghis Khan, 19–20
George Webb restaurants, 44–45
Germany, 20–22, 25
Gibson, Richard, 48
Gifford, Kathy Lee, 71
Glenwood Pines (Ithaca, New York), 57–58
Graham, Katherine, 77
Grapes of Wrath, The (Steinbeck), 25–26, 27
Gulf War, 90–91

Hall, Bridget, 90

Index

Hamburg, Germany, 20–22
Hamburger Hall of Fame (Seymour, Wisconsin), 86
Hamburger Helper, 15–16
hamburgers
  in Asia, 8, 59, 76, 94–96, 103–4
  immigration to U.S. and, 2–4, 20–22, 25
  industrial history of, 26–37
  kitsch objects, 85–87
  modern American, 22–26
  nonbeef variations, 7
  origins of, 19–22
  see also preparation methods; toppings
hamburger steak, 22
Happy Days (TV show), 93
Hardee, Wilber, 48
Hardee's, 13–15, 47–48
Hart, Gary, 85
Herbst, Sharon Tyler, 1
High Time (movie), 93
Hong Kong, 8, 76, 103–4
hot dogs, 47–48, 92
Hudson, Todd, 56–57
Hudson's (Coeur d'Alene, Idaho), 56–57

Iacocca, Lee, 78–79
Ingram, Edgar Waldo "Billy," 26–28
In-N-Out Burgers (California), 34
Insta-Burger King, 34–35
International Hamburger Hall of Fame (Daytona Beach, Florida), 86–87
Iowa 80 Restaurant (Walcott, Iowa), 52, 65
Irving, Bob, 2

Jack in the Box, 105
Jamison, Bill and Cheryl Alters, 66–67, 69
Java House (San Francisco), 58–59
JoAnn's Cafe (San Francisco), 104
Jollibee's (Daly City, California), 59
Jughead, 88

Karcher, Carl N., 47–48
Karlgaard, Rich, 76
Kentucky Fried Chicken, 39–40
Knoedl, Mary Lee, 59
Kroc, Ray, 31–34, 76, 83–85
Kuralt, Charles, 101–3

Lassen, Louis, 25
Letterman, David, 47
Levitt, Theodore, 32–34
Llamas, Connie, 101
Love, John F., 11, 22
Lowenstein, Roger, 76–78
Lucas, George, 93

Malloy, Sandy, 54
Manes, Stephen, 75
Mariani, John, 2
Marriott Corp., 43–44
McDonald, Maurice, 31–34
McDonald, Richard, 31–34
McDonald, Ronald L., 19–22
McDonald's, 2, 48
  in Asia, 59, 76, 94–96, 103–4
  Big Mac, 42–43, 71
  Disney and, 83–85
  founding of, 31–34
  industrial production of, 32–34
  mascots, 31, 95–97
  minimalist philosophy, 31–32
  publicity stunt in Germany, 22
  sales statistics, 11, 12–13, 16, 91–92
McGarvey, Mike and Tom, 58
McLamore, James, 34–37
McLaughlin, Maureen, 44
memorabilia, hamburger, 85–87
Menches, Frank, 25
Microsoft, 74, 75–76
milk shakes, 31, 61, 101
Miller, Tom, 100–101
models, 89–90
Mondale, Walter, 85
Mongols, 19–20
Montgomery, Nelle and Gordon, 60
music, 45–47, 81–83

Nagreen, Charlie ("Hamburger Charlie"), 22–25
National Cattlemen's Beef Association, 13
Newman, Paul, 66, 67, 69
Newman's Own, Inc., 67
New York City, 22, 61–62, 88, 92
New York Yankees, 92

O'Neill, Molly, 25, 65–66, 67, 71
onion rings, 69
Operation Desert Shield and Desert Storm, 90–91

Pagonis, William "Gus," 90–91
Patton, Phil, 4, 16
Peel, Terry, 52, 65
Peller, Clara, 85
Philbin, Regis, 71
Philippines, 59
Popeye (movie), 88
preparation methods, 5, 26, 65–73
  creativity in, 54–56, 71–72
  doneness, 69
  double-deck burger, 42–43
  meat, 65–69

116

Index

side dishes, 69–71
  see also toppings
Presley, Elvis, 80, 81
Pulp Fiction (movie), 94
Purner, John F., 60

Rally's, 47
Reality Bites (movie), 94
Redlich, Tracy, 44–45
Red's Java House (San Francisco), 58–59
Reilly, Steve and Maria, 58
Robbins, Tom, 4
Rochemont, Richard de, 6
Root, Waverley, 6
Rushmore, Steve, 57–58

sales statistics, 11–16
    McDonald's, 11, 12–13, 16, 91–92
    preferences, 13
    regional, 15
    toppings, 12
Salisbury, James Henry, 22
Salisbury steak, 22
Sandy's, 48
Saturday Night Live (movie), 93
Segar, E. C., 87–88
Seymour, Wisconsin, 22–25, 86
side dishes, 69–71
size
    Burger King Whopper, 35–36
    Cassell's, 54
    Cotham's, 59
    creativity and, 71–72
    double-deck burger, 42–43
    Hardee's burgers, 13–15
    McDonald's, 16, 32
    optimum, 66–67
    Tommy's, 2
    Vincenzo's, 55
    World's Largest Hamburger, 22–25
Sperl, Harry, 86–87
Steinbeck, John, 25–26, 27
Stern, Jane and Michael, 56
Steve Miller Band, 82
supermodels, 89–90

Taiwan, 103–4
Tarantino, Quentin, 94
Tennyson, Jeffrey, 22, 25, 28, 43, 65–66, 67, 69, 86–87
Thomas, R. David "Dave," 38, 39–40, 41
Tommy's (Los Angeles), 54
Tommy's (McCloud, California), 2
toppings
    bacon, 13

BBQ sauce, 12
    cheese, 6, 12, 13–15, 42, 44, 47, 54, 76–77
    chili, 54
    chili peppers, 71
    ketchup, 4, 12, 48, 71
    lettuce, 4, 12, 42, 44, 53
    mayonnaise/salad dressing, 12, 13, 44, 53
    mustard, 12, 63
    onions, 4, 12, 13–15, 26, 56, 58–59
    pickles, 12, 56, 88–89
    pineapple, 59
    relish, 12, 26, 42
    sales statistics on, 12, 13
    tomatoes, 4, 12, 53, 54
    see also preparation methods
Torre, Joe, 92
Trager, James, 25
Trellis Restaurant (Williamsburg, Virginia), 5
Trillin, Calvin, 51, 60–61
truck stops, 52, 65
Turner, Fred, 11
'21' Club (New York City), 61–62, 71

The Varsity (Atlanta), 53
Vincenzo's (Louisville, Kentucky), 54–56
Vlasic Foods, 88–89

Water Tower (Chicago), 28
Watson, James L., 94
Websites, White Castle testimonials, 28–31
Wendy's, 41
    founding of, 39–40
    "Where's the beef?" campaign, 85
When They Were Kings (movie), 105
White Castle, 26–31
    founding of, 26–28
    imitators, 28
    Website of testimonials, 28–31
White Hut (West Springfield, Massachusetts), 57–58
Wian, Bob, 40–44
Williams, Hank, Jr., 82–83
Wimpy, 87–88
Wimpy's Grills (Bloomington, Indiana), 88
Winstead, Katherine, 60
Winstead's (Kansas City, Missouri), 50, 60–61, 100–101
Wolf, Wesley, 91
World's Fair 1904 (St. Louis), 24, 25
World's Largest Hamburger, 22–25
Wu, David Y. H., 103–4

Yan, Yunxiang, 94–96, 103
Yancey, Lovie, 45

Zandl, Irma, 85

ABOUT THE AUTHOR

DAVID GRAULICH writes a nationally syndicated humor column, performs regular commentaries on National Public Radio, and is most recently the author of *Dial 9 to Get Out!*, a humorous look at office life. An avid and enthusiastic fan of hamburgers, french fries, and hot dogs, he resides with his family in San Bruno, California.